One Body,

One Spirit, and

One New Man

Witness Lee

Living Stream Ministry
Anaheim, CA

First Edition, June 2000.

ISBN 0-7363-0944-6

Published by

Living Stream Ministry
2431 W. La Palma Ave., Anaheim, CA 92801 U.S.A.
P. O. Box 2121, Anaheim, CA 92814 U.S.A.

Printed in the United States of America

00 01 02 03 04 05 / 9 8 7 6 5 4 3 2 1

CONTENTS

PREFACE

This book is a translation of messages given in Chinese by Brother Witness Lee during an international training in Taipei in October 1977. These messages were not reviewed by the speaker.

CHAPTER ONE

THE SPIRIT AND THE BODY

Scripture Reading: Eph. 4:4a; 1:23; 1 Cor. 12:13, 12

In these messages we will consider the one Body and the one Spirit. We all know that in Ephesians 4 there are two great matters: One is the Body, and the other is the Spirit. Because in the church many of you have received much help and have had many experiences, you know what I am talking about when I speak of one Body and one Spirit. However, if someone in today's Christianity were here and heard these terms, *one Body* and *one Spirit,* he may ask, "There are thousands of bodies here. How can there be only 'one Body'? And what kind of spirit is the 'one Spirit'? Does this refer to man as 'the spirit of all creation' or perhaps to a kind of cure-all?" If such a one thinks in this way and begins to roll his eyes, the speaker on the platform is not able to continue his message. This is truly the case.

However, the Lord is always with the spirit of the speaker. While I am speaking, in my spirit I can understand your situation. Even though you have no outward expression to tell me whether you are opposing my words or receiving them joyfully, I know your considerations. The spirit of the speaker is very sensitive. I do understand that you need some foundation in order to understand what the Body and the Spirit are, of which we are speaking here.

On your side, your heart should be pure, your spirit open, and your entire being ready to receive. If this is the case, then there will be a deep calling unto deep between you and me. The things within me will be able to flow out, and also the things within you will be able to flow out. In this way what should be released will be released.

Ephesians 4:4a speaks of "one Body and one Spirit." Is it correct to say "one Spirit and one Body?" Absolutely not, because in this verse *Body* is mentioned first. According to our understanding, we may ask, "Is the Spirit not greater and higher than the Body?" Yes, the Spirit is higher. Then why is the Body mentioned first and the Spirit second? This is because the topic of Ephesians 4 is not the Spirit but the Body. In other words, the entire book of Ephesians with all its six chapters is particularly on the Body. The Body is the subject, and the Spirit is the content of the subject. This is why chapter four speaks first of the Body and then of the Spirit. The Body and the Spirit are two great matters.

JESUS' RESURRECTION AND GLORIFICATION BRINGING THE SPIRIT INTO BEING

Before the day of Pentecost recorded in Acts 2, and before the resurrection and ascension of the Lord Jesus, did the Body exist in the universe? No, because at that time the church was not yet there. The Body is the church. Before the day of Pentecost there was no church, so there was no Body. We speak of one Body and one Spirit. It is very clear that the Body was not there before Pentecost, but before Pentecost and before the resurrection and ascension of the Lord Jesus, was *the Spirit* there? No, for John 7:39 says, "But this He said concerning the Spirit, whom those who believed into Him were about to receive; for the Spirit was not yet, because Jesus had not yet been glorified." The Spirit of God was there, but *the Spirit* was not yet.

To explain this we can use the illustration of making tea. If I have only a cup of plain water without any tea in it, I can say, "At this time the tea is not yet." There is water, but there is no tea yet. If I put tea leaves into the water, and after a minute or two the element of the tea has dissolved into the water, then there is tea. Five minutes ago there was water but no tea; now there is not only water but also tea.

Before the Lord Jesus resurrected and ascended, the Spirit of God was there, but we may compare Him to plain water. Then what is the "tea"? Figuratively speaking, the tea is the Lord Jesus in His humanity passing through death, entering into resurrection, being glorified, and being exalted. At this juncture, the whole process of the Lord Jesus being mingled with the Spirit of God was completed, just as tea is mingled with plain water. Thus, before the Lord Jesus was resurrected, the Spirit was not yet. This is not my view; this is what John 7:39 says. Furthermore, this verse explains why the Spirit at that time was not yet. It was because Jesus had not yet been glorified.

When was the Lord Jesus glorified? He entered into glory when He resurrected. The record in Luke 24 tells us that after His resurrection and before His ascension, when He met the two disciples on the road to Emmaus, the Lord told them, "Was it not necessary for the Christ to suffer these things and enter into His glory?" (v. 26). This proves that when He resurrected, even though He had not yet ascended, He had already entered into His glory.

What does it mean for the Lord Jesus to be glorified? Originally, the Lord Jesus was the God of glory, but in His incarnation He put on humanity. The flesh and the humanity that He had put on did not have a single bit of glory; in this sense, they were like our own flesh and humanity. But the God of glory, or we can say the glory of God, was within Him. Then one day, He was crucified and broken on the cross, buried in the grave, and He came out of death; this was the time of the release of the glory within Him. Furthermore, His body, which had passed through incarnation, death, and burial, now was fully saturated with His glory to become completely transformed, transfigured, and uplifted. Thus, after His resurrection He bore a transformed, transfigured, and uplifted human body and human nature. At that time, the humanity He had put on entered into glory. "The Spirit was not yet, because Jesus had not yet been glorified"; this means that at that time His physical body, His humanity, had not yet entered into God's glory, but after He rose from the dead, this man, Jesus the Nazarene, entered into glory, and His body, His humanity, that He had put on, entered into glory. At this time the Spirit came into being.

Ephesians 4:4 says, "One Body and one Spirit." This Spirit is "the Spirit." *Spirit* here does not refer merely to the Spirit

of God; *Spirit* refers to "the Spirit." If I pour plain water on a
white handkerchief, it will not leave any stain of color, and
the handkerchief will remain white. If, however, I pour tea on
a white handkerchief, it will leave a round yellow mark.
Before the Lord Jesus died and resurrected, the Spirit of God
was purely the Spirit of God without the element of humanity
or the uplifted humanity, without the sweet death of the Lord
Jesus, and without the power of His resurrection. There was
only one element—divinity. After the Lord Jesus resurrected,
however, the elements of His humanity, His death, and His
resurrection all entered into the Spirit of God, and from that
time on the Spirit of God became "the Spirit." This is why the
term *the Spirit* is used throughout the New Testament. However, because the translators of the Chinese Bible were afraid
that people would not understand the meaning of the term
the Spirit, they translated it as *Holy Spirit* even though they
noted that the word *holy* was not in the original. Moreover,
they lost the word *the* in their translation. They thought the
word *the* was unimportant, never realizing that this word is
crucial. "The Spirit!" Thus, one Body and one Spirit.

If we want to see the Spirit, we must consider the holy
anointing ointment in Exodus 30. The holy anointing ointment
was made of olive oil (typifying the Holy Spirit) compounded
with four kinds of spices. These four kinds of spices typify the
Lord's humanity, His death, and His resurrection. After these
four spices were compounded into the olive oil, the olive oil was
no longer only oil; it was an ointment. This holy anointing ointment typifies the Spirit. If you consider the Spirit only in the
New Testament, you will not see many details, but when you
look at the Old Testament type, you can see the details. One
hin of olive oil was compounded with four kinds of spices. In
addition, there are details concerning the measure of the four
spices: The first kind and the last kind are of five hundred
shekels each, while the middle two are of two hundred
fifty shekels each. Added together they equal a total of three
units, each unit of five hundred shekels, indicating three units
of responsibility. This signifies the Triune God, of whom the
Second was broken.

ALL THE EXPERIENCES OF CHRIST
BEING IN THE SPIRIT

This holy anointing ointment as the Spirit is a great topic. Do not think that I am exaggerating; over the past fifty years, the Lord has led us to progress in our knowledge of the truth. I would like to give you an example to show the importance of the Spirit. Up until 1938 or 1939, whenever Brother Watchman Nee spoke on Romans 6 he emphasized "reckoning" according to the light that we had up to that time. We "reckon" ourselves dead, and we "reckon" ourselves alive. He translated into Chinese a hymn written by A. B. Simpson, the founder of The Christian and Missionary Alliance. That hymn says, "Let us reckon, reckon, reckon...Let us reckon ourselves to be dead to sin...Let us reckon ourselves as alive in Him" (*Hymns*, #692).

In the summer of 1935, Brother Nee came to Chefoo, my hometown, and spoke a message in which he gave an illustration. He said that three persons were walking along the top of a wall. The first one was Fact, the second was Faith, and the third was Experience. Whenever Faith did not look to either side or to the back but kept going on, constantly looking at Fact, then Experience would not have a problem but would follow after him. But whenever Faith wavered and turned back to look at Experience, they all fell off the wall. Therefore, he said that we must have reckoning faith. The Lord Jesus already died on the cross and already crucified our flesh. These are facts, good news of great joy. Today you should have faith welling up in you because of God's word. This faith does not look from side to side or to the rear but always gazes at the fact. When you keep looking by faith, the experience will follow, and that experience is the experience of death.

Brother Nee's speaking was powerful, and we were very moved when we heard it. However, when we tried to put it into practice, we simply could not reckon ourselves dead. Before we tried to reckon ourselves dead, our flesh seemed to be sleeping; once we tried to reckon ourselves dead, it woke up and became more living. Between 1935 and 1938 Brother Nee frequently spoke on this topic, and from 1935 we tried to learn how to reckon ourselves dead, but year after year we were unable to do it. This continued until 1939 when Brother Nee returned from Europe and unexpectedly released a message in a meeting in Shanghai. That message was so different from what he had spoken before that it shocked me, yet it was a great help to me.

He said that the fact of our co-death with Christ that we see in Romans 6 can be experienced only in the Spirit found in Romans 8. You can never have the experience of the fact of being crucified with Christ in Romans 6 unless you are in the Spirit in Romans 8. In other words, it does not depend on your believing or reckoning; it depends only on your being in the Spirit. Without Romans 8 you can never have the experience of Romans 6. Romans 6 can only be a fact to you; it can never become your experience unless you live in the Spirit in Romans 8. At that time I wondered whether Brother Nee's present speaking was different from his previous speaking. It seemed to be different, but it was not truly different; it was a word of experience.

We need to reckon; Paul also reckoned. Nevertheless, we should not merely reckon in our mind without living in the Spirit. For example, your wife may provoke you, and you may be about to lose your temper. You will then feel that you must reckon yourself dead; you must reckon that the "I" who loses his temper has been crucified on the cross, and you must reckon him dead. But I must tell you that before you finish your reckoning, the devil may come to taunt you by saying, "You cannot make it to reckon yourself dead." Then you give up reckoning and your temper comes out. We have all experienced this.

Hence, it is not a matter of reckoning but a matter of living in the spirit and walking according to the spirit, that the righteous requirement of the law might be fulfilled in us, who do not walk according to the flesh but according to the spirit (Rom. 8:4). The mind set on the flesh is death, but the mind set on the spirit is life and peace (v. 6). When Brother Nee released this message, I received much help, and I had a turn in my knowledge of the Spirit. From that day on I knew that strictly speaking any word of preaching which does not have the Spirit is useless. This is because the word preached is like a prescription, but a prescription must be filled by the pharmacist before it can be useful. If you do not get the medicine, a prescription from the most famous doctor will be useless. The word is like the prescription, and the Spirit is like the medicine. It is not the prescription but the medicine that works. The high preaching cannot save you, but the Spirit can save you. Therefore, we all need this Spirit.

However, at that time I had not yet seen the different aspects of the Spirit, that this Spirit today is not only the Spirit of God but also the Spirit of Jesus, the Spirit of the One who suffered death in crucifixion. This Spirit is also the Spirit of Christ, the Spirit of the One who rose from the dead. This Spirit is also the Spirit of Jesus Christ, that is, the all-inclusive Spirit. The Spirit's moving within us is the anointing mentioned in 1 John 2, which is typified by the holy anointing ointment in Exodus 30.

By the Lord's grace, I can boast to you that the words I am speaking to you have not come at all from study in my mind. I can testify that every point was learned through my personal, painful experience. The conclusion is that we must have the Spirit. If you are not in the Spirit, every word of preaching will be empty and ineffective, but if you are in the Spirit, the reality will be there. You will see that it is a matter of one Body and one Spirit.

THE CHURCH BEING ONE BODY

Now we may speak something concerning the one Body. When I was young, I heard the preaching of the fundamentalists, and I also read their books. They said that the New Testament employs many figures of speech to portray the church, such as a wife and a body. They also said that this does not mean that the church is actually a wife or a body but that the church is only likened to a wife or a body. At that time, I listened to what they said and felt that it was logical, but gradually I discovered in my experience that the church as a body is not merely a figure of speech; the church today is indeed the Body. The New Testament does not say that the church as a body is a figure of speech. Rather, it says that we who are many are one Body. We are one Body!

When I was young, I often listened to an old English missionary preaching his favorite sermon: Love one another. Sometimes he would even discontinue coming to the Lord's table for a period of time because he felt that we were not loving one another and that we would have to love one another before we could break the bread. I heard the teaching of loving one another many times. But, brothers and sisters, today it is not simply a matter of loving one another. You must also know that we are members one of another. Let me use our body as an illustration. Suppose that the arms do not love the shoulders and the hands do not love the arms, or suppose that the arms regret being under the shoulders and the hands lament being under the arms. The Lord may say, "It is too late for regrets, because the hand is the hand and the arm is the arm. Whether you like it or not, you are what you are. It is not up to you; rather, it is according to My arrangement."

I do not believe that there are two people on earth today who can love each other until eternity without ever at some time disliking each other. Even, which husband and wife who truly love each other can testify that he or she has never found the other unlovable? I can testify that in one day my feelings can change many times: at six in the morning I may feel my wife is lovable, while ten minutes later I may feel she is unlovable, but after fifteen minutes I will love her again. Thus, loving one another is not very reliable. The Bible speaks not only of loving one another but also of being members of one another. Those who love one another are members one of another; those who do not love one another are still members one of another. Even if they gnash their teeth, the fact remains that they are still members one of another; there is no alternative. According to the way of the worldly people, if a husband and wife do not love each other, they get a divorce, but the hand and the arm can never be divorced. Today we not only love one another; we are also members one of another.

We must see what the church is. The church is the Body, and there is only one Body. You need light and revelation to see that the church is the Body. On the earth today there is

Christianity, but that is not the Body. There are those who love the Lord, but that is not the Body. There are those who are well-cultivated, but that is not the Body. There are those who pursue spirituality, but that is not the Body. What the Lord wants today is not your spirituality or your cultivation; He wants the Body. There is only one Body. Brothers and sisters, I can assure you that, unless there is a substantial expression of the Body, the Lord Jesus will never return. The Lord said, "I come quickly," but He has not yet returned. Why? Because the Body is not here; because the Body has not yet been manifested on the earth.

THE BODY NEEDING TO BE EXPRESSED
IN EACH LOCALITY

In conclusion, I am very happy to see many young working people in the Taipei district, and I would tell you that your responsibility is great. In addition, almost all the ones from Southeast Asia who have come to attend this conference and training are young people. This is a good sign, and I would like to say also to you that your responsibility is great. Since the gospel has been preached all over the earth today, it is hard to find a city that is without the gospel. There are thousands, tens of thousands, even millions of Christians on the earth, yet there is no Body. There are tens of thousands of Christians on the island of Taiwan, but with the exception of the small expression in the Lord's recovery, you cannot see the Body among any group of Christians. You can talk to them about the Holy Father, the Holy Son, and the Holy Spirit, and they will understand you, but if you talk to them about *the Spirit,* they will not understand. Therefore, brothers and sisters, we must pray for the day to come when our eyes will be opened and we will know what the Spirit is and what the Body is. We must bear a testimony on the earth and in the universe that there is only one Body. One Body and one Spirit—we must bear this testimony. We should not testify only in a big city such as Taipei, but we should also go to testify this in the towns and small cities with a population of 10,000 or 20,000. One Body and one Spirit—how glorious this is!

I hope that one day on the island of Taiwan, there will be a lampstand in each of the three hundred sixty large and small cities and towns. Perhaps some localities will have only twenty, thirty, or fifty brothers and sisters, but every town and every city will have a golden lampstand bearing the same testimony—one Body and one Spirit. That will be splendid! That could be the day of the Lord's coming.

I believe that today this testimony is on your shoulders, and you must bear this testimony as you return to your localities. You need to testify to this. You should not merely preach the gospel to get people saved; neither should you merely bring people to know life and understand the Bible. Rather, all of you must testify that there is one Body and one Spirit. We all live by this Spirit, and we all are the one Body.

MESSAGE TWO

THE FULLNESS AND THE BODY

Scripture Reading: Eph. 1:23; Gal. 3:27-28; Rom. 12:5; 1 Cor.
12:12; Acts 9:4-5; 1 Cor. 1:13a

THE BODY BEING THE FULLNESS
OF THE ONE WHO FILLS ALL IN ALL

In this message we will speak directly about the Body.
We must first ask, "What is the Body?" We may say that
there is only one verse in the entire New Testament that tells
us what the Body is, and that is Ephesians 1:23: "Which [the
church] is His Body, the fullness of the One who fills all in
all." The phrase *the fullness of the One who fills all in all* is
very difficult to understand and explain. Of course, we all
know that *the One who fills all in all* refers to the unlimited
Christ. Here *all* is used twice, successively, once referring
to Christ's filling all and another time referring to Christ's
being in all. *All* comprises all persons, all matters, and all
things and includes every person, every matter, and every
thing. In Greek, the word for *all* is *pan,* encompassing
persons, matters, and things. It is not wrong to translate that
Christ is "the One who fills all in all," but the meaning is
very broad. After studying this phrase for many, many years,
I still do not understand it. According to its meaning, *all* is
the correct translation, but according to its usage, it is very
difficult to understand.

Some people have translated this verse as "the fullness of
the One who fills all people in all people." This translation is
also correct, and it is easy to explain and apply. Christ truly
is the One who fills all people and is in all people. *All people*
does not refer to the unsaved; instead, it refers to all those

who belong to Him. This is similar to Colossians 3:11: "Where there cannot be Greek and Jew...but Christ is all and in all." *All* here is the same as *all* in Ephesians 1:23. Hence, the translation of this word requires a great deal of consideration. At this time I do not want to use the broad explanation of *all* because it is too difficult to define accurately. I want to use the narrow definition of this word and thus explain it as referring to all men, to all of us.

The church is the Body of Christ, the fullness of the One who fills all men in all men. All of us saved ones, as the members of Christ, are the "all men" mentioned here. Christ is in all of us, and He fills every one of us. Therefore, what is the church? The church is the Body of Christ. What is the Body? The Body is the fullness that issues from Christ's filling us within. Simply stated, the Body is the fullness of Christ. The church is the Body of Christ, and this Body is His fullness. To say that the Body is the fullness is very meaningful.

Suppose we have a strong, husky brother here who does not have a body but who only has a head hanging in the air. Even though his head is very big, he is without a body. Would you consider him full or not? He is not full; rather, he is poor and empty. We must know that the fullness of a person is not in his head but in his body. A person's body is his fullness. The Body of Christ is the fullness of Christ. Do not forget that Ephesians 1:23 says, "[The church] is His Body, the fullness of the One who fills all in all." In brief, the Body of Christ is the fullness of Christ. Where is this Christ? This Christ is the One who fills all the saints in all the saints. His Body is the issue of such a filling.

THE FULLNESS OF CHRIST
COMING FROM THE RICHES OF CHRIST

Now we must go one step further to see where the fullness comes from. When a brother is born, he is just a little baby who is not so full. How then does he become so full? It is by eating. He eats chicken, beef, bread, and other things for many months and many years. Then all the food as the riches are assimilated and constituted into his organic body to become his fullness.

In the past seventeen or eighteen years I have stated several times the fact that Ephesians chapter one and chapter four both mention fullness, while chapter three mentions the riches of Christ. What is the difference between the riches of Christ and the fullness of Christ? Please remember that if you put a big pile of food here, it would not be called fullness; it would be called riches. However, once you have eaten these riches item by item and have digested them, they become your cells and the elements of your body. Consequently, your body is constituted with what you have eaten and digested. This constituted body is a fullness. After the riches have been digested and constituted into a body, they become the fullness of the body. The riches of Christ are boundless, immeasurable, and unsearchable, but you still need to eat and assimilate these riches of Christ. The more Christ you eat and the more Christ is assimilated into you, the more element of the fullness you will gain. I believe that you all are clear what the fullness of Christ is. It is Christ experienced by you, assimilated by you, and constituted into your being to become your element; this is the fullness, which is the Body of Christ.

NOT BEING THE NATURAL MAN
BUT THE MAN RECONSTITUTED WITH CHRIST

Someone may say, "Since I am a believer, I am a member of Christ." Generally speaking, this saying is right. Strictly speaking, however, as a natural man, you are not a member of Christ. It is only when the life of Christ, the nature of Christ, and everything of Christ have entered your being to regenerate and reconstitute you that you become a member of Christ. Originally you were altogether a natural person and not a member of Christ. In order to be a member of Christ you must be reconstituted. How can you be reconstituted? Christ has to enter into you to regenerate you, and He has to continue to enter into you, to dispense His element into you, in order to constitute you. As a result, your entire being, from the inside to the outside, will pass through a process of thorough reconstituting, so that you will no longer be what you were originally, but you will be a regenerated and transformed person. Only this regenerated, transformed person can be a member of Christ.

The Body of Christ is the fullness of Christ, and the fullness of Christ is the issue of our being constituted with the riches of Christ which we have enjoyed. At this point His riches are no longer objective but subjective. The objective riches have become the subjective fullness; this is the Body of Christ. The Body is this fullness. Therefore, Colossians 3 and Galatians 3 say that in this Body there cannot be Jew and Greek.

Suppose there is a Jew here, and there is also a Greek, a Gentile. The Jew was born a Jew and the Greek was born a Greek, but now they have both believed in the Lord Jesus; their sins have been forgiven, and they have been saved. Nevertheless, their original Jewish and Greek persons have not yet been touched, so one is still a Jew and the other is still a Greek. When they come together, can you say that here there is neither Jew nor Greek? No, you cannot because both the Jew and the Greek are still here.

When I was young, I read Colossians 3 and Galatians 3, which say that there cannot be Jew and Greek, and I said, "How could this be! I am a Chinese who has believed in Jesus, and I have been saved for four or five years; how can I say that I am not a Chinese? I am still a Chinese!" Gradually, I understood and realized that each of us saved ones has a dual status: the outward status which is our old status and the inward status which is our new status. According to our outward status, there are Chinese, Germans, British, Americans, and even some Jews among us. In our natural being we are certainly these people. As we come together, if everyone still lives in his natural being, can we say that this is the Body of Christ? No, we cannot because in the Body of Christ there is neither Jew nor Greek.

Today we must know the revelation of God to such an extent that we see that the church is the Body of Christ and that this Body is not our natural man. Our natural being is not a constituent of this Body. Galatians 3:28 even says that there cannot be male and female. These words were not

written by me; they were written by Paul and are the words
of the Bible. Galatians 3:27 says, "As many of you as were
baptized into Christ have put on Christ." This sentence is not
very simple. The first meaning of baptism is burial, and its
second meaning is resurrection. To be buried is to put off
something, while to be resurrected is to put on something.
What are we putting off in our burial? We are putting off our
natural man: the Jew and the Greek, the free man and the
slave, the male and the female. The person you were formerly
was buried in your baptism. I would ask you, "Have you truly
been buried?" If you have been buried, then leave your former
person in the grave. This is the putting off. This is the first
aspect of the significance of baptism. The second aspect of its
significance is resurrection, which is a putting on. What are
we putting on? We are putting on Christ. In Greek, to put on
Christ is to be clothed with Christ. We who were baptized
into Christ have put on Christ. We put off the natural man
and buried him in the tomb. Then we put on something new,
which is Christ. In this Christ, whom we have put on, there is
neither Jew nor Greek, neither slave nor free man, neither
male nor female, because we all have become one. This is the
church, and this is the Body.

The condition of most Christians today is very different
from this. They are not in this oneness but in so many other
things. Today in the Lord's recovery, however, we all need to
see that we can let go of everything, but we cannot let go of
this oneness, which is Christ. We have clearly seen that the
Body of Christ is the fullness of Christ, which comes out of
our enjoyment of the riches of Christ. Therefore, the fullness
is Christ Himself enjoyed by us, assimilated by us, and constituted into us as our element. This fullness is absolutely
subjective to us. We may say that the riches of Christ are
objective and outside of us, but the fullness of Christ is
altogether subjective to us and is in the element of our entire
being. This means that when we are the Body of Christ, it is
no longer we, but it is Christ who lives in us, just as Galatians
2:20 says, "I am crucified with Christ; and it is no longer I
who live, but it is Christ who lives in me." When we allow
Christ to live in us, we have put Him on and have put off our

old man, our natural man. We have put on Christ Himself. It is in this Christ that we all are one. It is in this Christ that we all are His Body, His fullness. It is in this "oneness," this fullness, that there is no natural man: no Chinese, no foreigner, no Honanese, no Hopeinese, no male, and no female. In this fullness everything is Christ.

THE LORD'S RECOVERY BEING THE RECOVERY OF THE ONENESS OF THE BODY

The Lord's recovery today is mainly a recovery of the oneness of the Body. It is not a recovery of a certain truth or of a certain doctrine; the Lord's recovery today is a recovery of this oneness in Christ. Hence, if we see this vision, this revelation, then we will not have any arguments about anything. You will not say that you disagree with foot-washing, neither will I say that I disagree with head covering. These both will become topics of little significance. You need to see that we both have been baptized into Christ and that in this baptism our old creation, our natural being, and our former person have all been buried and put off. Today we are living in Christ and by Christ. We are one here, and nothing can touch us. We are one not only with Christ, but we are also one with one another in Christ. We are not one in anything outside of Christ; we are one in Christ. We are one not because we all have the same doctrine or opinion. No, we are one because we all are in Christ. Our mentality, our thoughts, and our opinions may be different, but by the Lord's grace we all must deny these differences. Are you for head covering? You must tell the Lord, "O Lord, I let head covering go!" Are you for foot-washing? You must tell the Lord, "O Lord, I let foot-washing go!" In the same principle, do you like to pursue spirituality? I hope you will also have the boldness to tell the Lord, "O Lord, I will let even spirituality go! I want to live in this 'oneness.' What I need is not head covering, foot-washing, holiness, or spirituality; I care only for this 'oneness,' this one Body."

When I was between the ages of twenty and twenty-five, I read a little of the Bible, gained some knowledge of the Bible, and was very particular about biblical doctrines. I tried to do everything according to the biblical doctrines. At that time, I saw some people who took the Lord's supper by cutting up pieces of bread, and I condemned them greatly. Moreover, whenever I met someone, I would always ask how he was baptized. Was it by sprinkling or by immersion? If it was by sprinkling, I would say that was not right; it had to be by immersion. I ask you, Was it right for me to do that? It is hard to answer. From the standpoint of doctrines, it was right because we all need to be scriptural. Please remember, however, that from the standpoint of the Body, it was wrong. Why? Even if we have only a few words of argument concerning sprinkling and immersion, the Body is divided. Gradually, by the Lord's grace, I came to know that sprinkling is not a main issue. This is not to say that today I agree with sprinkling but to say that this is not an important point. The important thing is that someone is in Christ and that he lives in Christ. Today we must abandon the doctrinal disputes of the last four hundred years since Luther's Reformation.

I would say a little more on this. In 1968 among us there were numerous times when many brothers and sisters jumped into the water to be buried. When news of this went out, there were rumors that I was speaking heresy, teaching multiple baptisms. Actually, I myself did not get buried because I did not feel that there was any oldness in me that needed to be buried. I did expect from the beginning that the opposers would oppose this; however, this is not my point. My point is that whether you have been baptized once or twice, regardless of how many times you have been baptized, if you are still living by your natural life, if you are still you, then your baptism is not effectual. As long as you still live by your natural life, there is no value in getting baptized or in not getting baptized; it is worthless to be baptized once and likewise worthless to be baptized many times. The entire matter does not rest upon this kind of issue. Today in the Lord's recovery we all must be delivered from doctrinal arguments. If you are still stuck in these matters, it proves that you have not yet seen what the Body is.

Please do not misunderstand me. I am not saying that you should not be baptized, nor am I saying that when you are baptized it is all right for you to be baptized by sprinkling. I would say absolutely that according to the Bible you should be baptized by immersion, but you should not consider this a major topic. I have seen that some people are very particular about baptism. Some say you must be baptized forward, while others say you must be baptized sideways. If we are still paying attention to these methods of baptism, it proves that our eyes are darkened and we have not seen the light. These things do not matter; what matters is that you are a person living in Christ and not living according to your natural person. If you are living in Christ, whether you are baptized forward, backward, or sideways is all right. Some people would argue with me and say, "Since this is the case, then we do not need to be baptized." This also is too much, because the Bible clearly tells us, "He who believes and is baptized shall be saved" (Mark 16:16). Baptism is necessary, but when we baptize, we do not need to be so particular in letter about the ways of baptism. Therefore, you should never argue. This is true about any matter.

When I was young, I also thoroughly studied the matter of the sisters covering their heads. I studied this matter to such an extent that I looked even into the color, size, style, thickness, and material of the covering, and I even studied how it should be worn. Strictly speaking, the coverings used by the sisters today are all inadequate; I do not agree with any of them. However, I do not care for these things. I attended a month of meetings in London and saw that the hats worn by the Christian women in England were different one from the other, and they were of diverse, new styles. That is not covering one's head; that is being fashionable. Nevertheless, I was not bothered, and I still fellowshipped with them because I did not care for these things. Whoever has been baptized into Christ has put on Christ. It does not matter how many times one has been baptized, nor does it matter what style of head covering one wears; living Christ is what matters. This is why there has not been any dispute among us in these past several years. Only those who have not seen the Body of Christ would pay attention to these matters. Those who have seen the Body do not care for these things. What is the Body?

It is the fullness of Christ. What is the fullness of Christ? It is your inward enjoyment and experience of Christ; it is your living in Christ and your allowing Christ to live in you. This is the Body.

The matters I have spoken about here are very shallow, but now I would like to describe a few deeper matters. Some pursue holiness, some pursue spirituality, and some even pursue the subjective experience of Christ. Nevertheless, I would like to say that you must be delivered even from pursuing the subjective experience of Christ. What the Lord wants is not merely the subjective experience but the church that is produced through the subjective experience. What the Lord wants is the church. If your subjective experience makes you so individualistic that you cannot be blended with others, then that is a big mistake. Everything is good about you, and this is right. However, this is not the final test; the final test is whether you can be blended with others. If your spirituality, your holiness, and your subjective experience make you individualistic, then you have to put a question mark on them. When a drop of water falls into water, it is immediately blended into that water. However, if a drop of oil falls into the water, it remains a drop of oil; it does not blend with the water even though it is in the water. According to value, oil is worth more than water, but in the overall picture, oil is troublesome. Some brothers are very good, yet they do not go along with the flow, get along with others, blend with others, or coordinate with others. I am afraid that this kind of brother will become a "good" problem. You are very good, yet you become a problem.

After visiting many places and observing many kinds of Christians in the past twenty-five years, my heart truly grieves. Those who love the world, love the world; those who love sin, love sin; those who do not know the flesh, do not know the flesh. Some, like the Pentecostals, play with the spiritual gifts. Moreover, the so-called spiritual ones cannot get along with one another. According to my observation, the more spiritual a person is, the more he does not get along with others. I once visited a so-called spiritual group and saw that all of them were individualistically spiritual, not getting along with one another and even criticizing others before my face. Their criticism of others was civil and polite, but the Holy Spirit did not confirm their speaking. This is the reason their work did not bear any fruit. Thus, today it is not a matter of how spiritual or how holy we are; it is a matter of the oneness, of the Body, of the fullness.

Dear brothers and sisters, we all need to have the grace and mercy to see the vision that it is not a matter of the interpretation of doctrines or even a matter of being spiritual and holy. Rather, it is a matter of Christ's living in us and of our living in Christ. It is a matter of there not being Jew and Greek, slave and free man, male and female, because we all are one in Christ. Nothing matters but this oneness. This is the Body.

Brothers and sisters, this is the testimony the Lord wants today. We need to go to every place to testify this one thing: We are one in Christ. Three of us coming together are one; thirty of us coming together are one; three hundred of us coming together are still one. We are one when we come together in one locality; we are still one when we come together from ten localities. When we come together from ten countries, we are one; when we come from all the countries, we are still one. This is the Body of Christ: one Body and one Spirit. I do not believe that we are all exactly the same, but I thank the Lord that we are one in spirit. Now, whenever anyone comes to speak to me about how to practice head covering or baptism, I do not have the heart to get into it. I would like to testify that I have been delivered from these matters. This does not mean that we do not do things according to the Bible. On the contrary, we do everything according to the Bible, but even more importantly, we walk according to the Spirit. Galatians 3:27-28 says, "For as many of you as were baptized into Christ have put on Christ. There cannot be Jew nor Greek, there cannot be slave nor free man, there cannot be male and female; for you are all one in Christ Jesus." It is here that we have to ask, "Is Christ divided?" No! We do not care for doctrines; we are the Body. The Body is Christ, and Christ cannot be divided.

THE PRACTICAL EXPRESSION OF THE BODY

Scripture Reading: Eph. 1:23; 4:10, 13

In these days I have been very happy because for many years I have been waiting for an opportunity to release some messages specifically concerning the Body of Christ. Now I feel that I have such a good opportunity for us to focus on the Body. If we do not know the Body well enough, we will never be able to thoroughly know the church. Until now, very few Christians have known what the church is. It is important that we all have a clear knowledge of the church.

LIVING BY CHRIST BEING THE ONLY WAY TO HAVE THE REALITY OF THE CHURCH

I must first paint a background. The worst kind of concept Christians have concerning the church is that the church is a chapel, to consider that a building, a chapel, is the church. We all know that this is a great mistake. This kind of knowledge is not even worth mentioning, and we can throw it aside. The Brethren rose up in the last century to strongly teach that a chapel, as a building for worship, is not the church. They told people that the church is not a place but a group of people. They found the light in the New Testament to prove that the church is a gathering together of the redeemed ones. In Greek the word for church means the gathering together of the called-out ones. On the surface it is right to say that the church is not a place or a hall but a gathering together of the ones called by God. Yes, such a gathering is the church.

There is, however, a problem here. I can describe it by means of an example. We may be a group of about one hundred people. All of us have been called, and we have the opportunity to gather together at this time. Of course, according to the letter, all of us gathered together are the church. However, suppose that none of us lives in the spirit, that all one hundred of us are living in one hundred different minds. Some are from Singapore with a Singaporean mind; some are from Tokyo with a Japanese mind; some are from Seoul with a Korean mind; and some are from Germany with a German mind. None of us knows what it means to live in the spirit. We all have our own opinions, our own views, and our own backgrounds; the only thing we have in common is that we have all believed in the Lord Jesus and have become Christians. With regard to our sins having been washed away by the precious blood, we all are the same. With regard to the Lord Jesus being our Savior, we also are the same. Concerning our belief of the Bible, we all are carrying the same Bible. We all say that we are those who belong to the Lord. Apparently we are the church when we gather together, but what about the reality of this? Three Christians may be totally French, another three are completely German, and another eight are wholly Singaporean. We all feel that our sins have been washed away, and we have been saved; we also feel that the Lord loves us, and we belong to Him. However, none of us lives in the spirit or by the Spirit. On the one hand, we are the church, but on the other hand, we cannot say that we are truly the church. We are not the church because we are all in our minds. Although we have Christ, our Christ is on the throne in the heavens and in our minds, but He is not in our spirit or in our living. We do not live by Christ, and we cannot say, "It is no longer I who live, but it is Christ who lives in me." Moreover, when we come together we cannot say that here there is no French, no German, no Singaporean, no Filipino but all are one in Christ. You can see that apparently we are the church, but in reality we are not at all the church.

It is true that we are the assembly of the called-out ones, and based on this we acknowledge that we are the church. In reality, however, we are not the Body of Christ. This word is hard. How can we say that we are the church but not the Body of Christ? I tell you that according to reality this is the case. Apparently, we are all Christians, and we are the church when we come together; however, from the viewpoint of the Body, we are not the Body of Christ, nor are we the fullness of Christ. Some of us are the fullness of France, some of us are the fullness of Germany, and some of us are the fullness of Singapore; but we are not the fullness of Christ.

THERE BEING NO BODY OF CHRIST WHEN WE LIVE BY THE FLESH OR THE NATURAL MAN

If you have this light and use it to carefully examine today's Christianity, you will say that the Body of Christ is nowhere to be found. The reason is the condition of today's Christianity. When I was young, I studied at an English-speaking college in Chefoo that was managed by the American Presbyterian Mission Board. I knew the situation with that mission board and the Presbyterian Church. The American Presbyterian Church sent some American missionaries, who also taught at my school. When these Western missionaries and the Chinese pastors of the Presbyterian Church held a meeting, they were clearly divided into two groups of people. The two sides frequently argued with each other, sometimes even throwing brush pens or Bibles at each other. Is this the Body? No, this is not the Body but the flesh. This is why I say that apparently it is the church, but in reality it is not. That was definitely not the church.

Do not forget, however, that while the situation among us is obviously stronger and better—when we come together, we do not have outward quarreling, nor do we throw pens at one another—we still have to go one step further to ask ourselves whether our meeting together is according to Christ in our spirit or according to something else. If instead of being according to Christ in our spirit, we are according to our meekness, our speech, our maneuvering, our diplomacy, or our clever answers, then in principle this is still the flesh. This is merely a slightly more civilized flesh, a more refined flesh.

In 1958 I went to a certain place in England and stayed there for one month. While I was there, they did not arrange for me to speak only at conferences; they also wanted me to speak in the Lord's Day meetings and other regular meetings. Two days before I was to leave, it was to be my final weekly evening meeting there, and I did not even consider that I would need to speak. When I walked into the meeting hall, however, their responsible brother came forward and said, "Brother Lee, we would still ask you to speak tonight." I said, "I have not even thought about doing this." He insisted that I speak, so I agreed. I had had no intention of speaking, nor was I prepared, but as I was going up to the platform, the burden came. I released a strong message, saying, "The ministry is for the local churches; the local churches are not for the ministry. Regardless of how experienced, how high, how rich, how spiritual, or how heavenly the ministry is— perhaps like the ministry of the apostle John, and regardless of how poor or how unbecoming the local churches are— maybe like five of the seven churches in Revelation chapters two and three, the ministry is still for the churches, and the churches are not for the ministry." The word I spoke that day hit the mark concerning their condition. They were altogether for having the meetings for the ministry instead of having the ministry for the meetings.

My point is that when I was staying there, not one of them was wild; instead, they were all very civil and refined. Yet each of them would make an appointment to come talk with me in the room where I was staying and use that time to criticize others in a very refined way. They were not barbaric; rather, they were all very proper. That was the refined flesh, not the Body. Do we want that kind of refinement among us? We do not. That is being diplomatically refined. It is like a situation in which behind the scenes the airplanes and can-nons are all ready for war while the diplomats are still here shaking hands with one another. I am describing these things to show you that today's Christians do not have the Body.

What is the Body? The Body is not merely a composition of a group of the called-out ones; the Body is the fullness of Christ. The Body is not only the expression of Christ but also the fullness of Christ. How does this fullness come into being? It is by your receiving the riches of Christ into you to be enjoyed and assimilated by you and even to become you. We may compare this to eating fish, chicken, and bread. After about five or six hours, they are digested into you to become you. It is at this time that you are the fullness.

At this time I have been in Taipei for more than ten days. Let us suppose that for the past seven days I did not eat any food or drink any water but instead I only laid in my bed at home. In this case you would have to carry me to the meeting, and as I stand all thin and pale, my whole body would be shaking. What would that be? That would not be the fullness. However, for these past ten days I have eaten the riches of Taiwan, including fish, chicken, and many other things; I have eaten a great amount of the riches of Taiwan, and these riches have been assimilated into me and have become me. Now, therefore, I can stand here full of life and energy. This is the fullness. The church is the fullness of Christ. This is what the Lord wants today.

THE LORD URGENTLY NEEDING
THE EXPRESSION OF THE BODY

Today the Lord has an urgent need on the earth. He needs the reality of the Body to be expressed in each locality. At this time, by the Lord's own doing, there are brothers and sisters gathered together here from six major continents of the world, representing at least eighteen countries. We are not conferring, negotiating, or bargaining. We are here for only one thing, that is, to be in spirit. What does it mean to be in spirit? To be in spirit is to be in Christ. Today the Lord needs this kind of testimony on the earth. In locality after locality, no matter how many people there are in the church life, all are one in spirit. "There cannot be Jew nor Greek, there cannot be slave nor free man, there cannot be male and female" (Gal. 3:28). Here there is only Christ. We all have become one in Christ. This is what the Lord wants today. This should not be the case only in one locality, but even when many localities come together, all are one. When Taipei, Taichung, Tainan, Kaohsiung, and Chiayi all come together, they are also one. Here there cannot be Taipei or Tainan; there cannot be Kaohsiung or Chiayi; there can only be Christ. In Christ we are all one. The same is true not only among a few localities, but even when many countries are gathered together. When all those from Indonesia, Singapore, Malaysia, the Philippines, Hong Kong, and Taiwan come together, they also should say, "There cannot be Indonesia or the Philippines; there cannot be Malaysia or Hong Kong; there cannot be Singapore or Taiwan. There can only be Christ." This is the Body which the Lord wants. The Body is not only local but also universal. In principle it is one, whether in its local aspect or in its universal aspect. Thus, we can all see that these few passages of the Bible are extremely demanding.

THE ALL-FILLING CHRIST NEEDING A GREAT BODY

"[The church] is His Body, the fullness of the One who fills all in all" (Eph. 1:23). This verse of the Bible is a great problem to the translators. Colossians 3:11 says, "Where there cannot be Greek and Jew, circumcision and uncircumcision, barbarian, Scythian, slave, free man, but Christ is all and in all." If you have a Greek Bible in your hands, you can compare these two verses. You will see that the same words are used in both verses. In Colossians 3:11, *all* refers to all the saints. In the new man, there cannot be Greek and Jew, and so on, but Christ is all the believers and in all the believers. According to this verse, Ephesians 1:23 should be translated: "...the One who fills all people in all people." However, if you continue your reading to Ephesians 4:10, you will see that there are still some particular details. There it says that the Lord Jesus first descended to the earth to be incarnated and then after His death and resurrection He ascended far above all the heavens. This ascension was "that He might fill all things." *All things* here and *all* in 1:23 are the same word in Greek, so it is not proper to translate it as "all people." We see in 4:10 that there is the earth as well as the heavens. Hence, it is not a matter only of people; it truly is a matter of all things. The reason that He first descended to the earth and then ascended above all the heavens was that He might fill all things. Therefore, according to Ephesians 4:10, Ephesians 1:23 should be translated, "the One who fills all things in all things." According to the meaning of the original language both translations are correct. If we go by the second translation, Christ today is the One who fills all things in the universe.

This universal Christ, the Christ who fills all things, the Christ who is both in the heavens and on the earth, needs a Body to be His fullness. When He was on earth as Jesus the Nazarene, He could not be in Judea at the same time He was in Galilee, nor could He be in Jerusalem when He was in Samaria. This was because He was a small Jesus. He was limited by His flesh. But what about today? He has risen from the dead and ascended to the heavens, so He fills all things. He can be in the heavens and on the earth simultaneously; He can be in one place in the heavens, and at the same time He can be in millions of places on the earth. He is such a One who fills all things, so He needs a great Body as His fullness. Thus, today we can say that because He has such a great Body on earth, He is in heaven and He is also in Taipei, in Hong Kong, in Manila, in Singapore, in London, in Germany, in the United States, in Africa, in North America, and in South America. His Body is everywhere. What is this Body? It is His fullness, His universal fullness.

Dear brothers and sisters, you should not merely listen to this word and take it as doctrine. You must see that today the actual church (I am not speaking of the genuine church alone but the practical, present church) is the fullness of Christ in each locality. In other words, the actual church today is a part of Christ. The church in Taipei is the part of Christ that is in Taipei. The church in Singapore is the part of Christ that is in Singapore. Christ today is not a local Christ but a universal Christ, and this universal Christ has a part of Himself in every locality. The part in Taipei is called the church in Taipei, the part in London is called the church in London, and the part in New York is called the church in New York. Every local church is a part of Christ. All these parts constitute the Body.

THE CONDITION OF THE CHURCH TODAY
LACKING THE REALITY OF THE BODY

But, and this is a big "but," suppose the brothers and

sisters in Los Angeles apparently are meeting in the name of the Lord as the church in Los Angeles, but when they live, they all live by their natural being, their flesh, their self, their individuality, and their peculiarities. If this is their condition, do you think the so-called "church in Los Angeles" is a part of Christ? No. Then what is it a part of? It is one hundred percent a part of Adam.

Next, let us talk about Hong Kong. In Hong Kong there are also some brothers and sisters who have seen the light; they are standing on the ground of locality and are meeting in the Lord's name. Are they the church? Yes, they are definitely the church. They have believed in the Lord and have been washed in the precious blood. They love the Lord very much, and they also love the brothers and sisters. However, what if they love only those brothers and sisters who suit their taste and "spit out" those who do not. As they are such a group of people, are they the church in Hong Kong? Yes, they truly are, but among them some brothers and sisters are still living entirely in their natural being, while others have a character that is harder than steel. They all live by their individualities, politics, cleverness, preferences, and peculiar dispositions. When they come together to meet, this one disapproves of that one, and that one disagrees with this one. They have all seen that for the sake of the local ground they have to meet together. Yet when they come together, they are not willing to drop their politics, individualities, dispositions, and preferences. Is this the Body? No! What is this? We may boldly say, "The flesh!"

Some brothers and sisters might say, "Brother Lee, your preaching is wrong. How can you say that the church is not the Body? Does not Ephesians 1 say that the church is His Body? Since the brothers and sisters in Hong Kong are the church, how can they not be the Body? How do you answer this?" Yes, in name they are the church, but in reality they are not the Body but the flesh.

In 1947 and 1948 I was in Shanghai, and Brother Nee was also in Shanghai. We often talked about the condition of the churches in the entire country. Sometimes we talked about certain people, and Brother Nee made a joke saying, "Those people have been saved but have not been regenerated." I said, "Brother Nee, this is not right according to truth. How can you say that a person has been saved without having been regenerated?" He also laughed at himself. He said, "Because they believe in the precious blood, they are saved. But ever since I have known them and contacted them many times, I have never touched their spirit. They believe in the Lord's name and His precious blood, and they also pray, but whenever I contact them, I can never touch their spirit. It seems as if they are saved but are without the Spirit; is this not being saved without being regenerated?" Doctrinally speaking, this cannot be. To be sure, a saved person is regenerated, and a regenerated person is surely saved; salvation and regeneration cannot be separated. However, you cannot deny that some have called on the Lord's name, believed in the cleansing of the Lord's blood, and confessed that they are Christians, yet you cannot touch their spirit. They have their views, opinions, skills, and devices; they can do everything, but they do not have the Spirit. Have you ever seen this kind of situation? In the same principle, there are places where the church is as if it has been saved without ever being regenerated. In some places the so-called church is the church without being the Body. In some places it is the church, but only fifteen percent is the Body while eighty-five percent is not. In some places it is the church, but only forty-five percent is the Body while fifty-five percent is not. Truly and strictly speaking, there is hardly any church that is one hundred percent the Body.

THE CHURCH BEING THE BODY, AND THE BODY BEING THE FULLNESS

What is the Body? The Body is the fullness of Christ. In doctrine the church is the Body, but as to reality there is still a question of how much element of the Body is there. Brothers and sisters, we should not condemn others; we must see our own condition. At this time we all must confess in the light of the Lord that even we ourselves up to this day may live only thirty percent by the Spirit, leaving seventy percent that we live by ourselves. Have you seen this? This is the

Lord's need today. The Lord does not merely need a church in each locality; He needs a Body. As soon as we do not live by Christ, as soon as we are not living by the Spirit, we are not the Body. In name we are still the church, but in reality we are not the Body. Why? Because the Body is the fullness of Christ.

Do not forget the word *is* in Ephesians 1:23: "[The church] *is* His Body, the fullness of the One who fills all in all." This means that the church *is* the Body, and the Body *is* the fullness. These two levels of "is" are in succession rather than in parallel. It is not that on the one hand the church is the Body, while on the other hand the church is the fullness. Rather, it is that the church is the Body, and the Body is the fullness. According to doctrine, the fullness equals the Body, and the Body equals the church. But according to reality, a man can be in the church and still not live in the Body. All the brothers and sisters who meet in Hong Kong are in the church, but who is living in the Body? This becomes a big question mark. Strictly speaking, that which can fulfill God's eternal purpose is not the church in name but the Body. The Body is the fullness of Christ. I repeat that if you look from this angle and measure with this yardstick, you will see that today on earth in the churches there is not much of the element of the Body.

THE NEED FOR THE MEASURE OF THE STATURE OF THE FULLNESS OF CHRIST

Ephesians 4:13 goes one step further; there is not only the fullness of Christ but also the measure of the stature of the fullness of Christ. The phrase *the measure of the stature* includes two concepts: one is the stature and the other is the measure of that stature. For example, if you look at Brother Chang, you can see that his stature is tall and big. This stature certainly has a measure. The combination of these two things is called "the measure of the stature." The fullness of Christ has a stature, and this stature has a measure. Simply speaking, it is called "the measure of the stature of the fullness of Christ." If Brother Chang stands before us, we can see his body. We all have learned to say that this body is the fullness of Brother Chang. Moreover, his fullness has a stature, and this stature has a measure. Let us say, for example, that he is six feet two inches tall and over two feet wide; this measure is the measure of his stature. This is called "the measure of the stature of the fullness."

However, let us suppose that Brother Chang has not yet arrived at the measure of the stature of his fullness and that he is only four feet five inches tall and fourteen inches across the shoulders. In this case you would see that there is a lack in him. When you read Ephesians 4:13, you can see that the church as the Body of Christ does not become full instantly; instead, it grows continually. Do not forget that 4:13 first says, "Until we all arrive...at a full-grown man." A full-grown man is a man with the measure of the stature of his fullness. Now Brother Chang is a full-grown man, a man with the measure of the stature of his fullness; he is six feet two inches tall and over two feet wide. However, has the church in Taipei today arrived at a full-grown man? It has not. Has the church in Taipei arrived at the measure of the stature of the fullness of Christ? It has not. Suppose the measure of the stature of the fullness of Christ is eighteen feet tall, but the church in Taipei is only nine feet tall. Then it still lacks one half the height.

Please remember that the shorter the measure of the stature of Christ is, the more opinions everyone has. The lack in the measure of the stature of the fullness of Christ indicates that the believers are more in their natural man. Once the believers stay in their natural man, they are full of opinions. Now the church in Taipei is "nine feet tall," but if in the next six months it grows to ten feet tall, that would mean that the natural aspect has been reduced by one foot. When the natural aspect reduces by one foot, then the spiritual aspect increases by one foot. If in another year the church is twelve feet tall and after another year it is thirteen feet tall, that would mean that the spiritual aspect has kept increasing while the natural aspect has kept decreasing.

In any case, the measure of the stature of the fullness is not attained in an instant; it needs to grow. We must grow! First this verse says that "we all arrive...at a full-grown

man," then verse 14 says that "we may be no longer little
children," and verse 15 says, "But holding to truth in love,
we may grow up into Him in all things, who is the Head,
Christ." This measure of the stature requires growth.

We all know that the measure of the stature of a child
needs growth. I have a small grandson who was born in
January of this year. When Sister Lee and I went to visit him,
he was pitifully small. But when we went again in October,
in those few months he had grown from a small baby to a
naughty little child who could greet us and make faces at
us. This little child grew much in just a few months. We
may illustrate our problem in this way: Some churches were
a certain height when I visited them ten years ago. Then
on a visit eight years ago they had shrunk a little, and on
another visit three years ago they had grown about one-half
of an inch, but on my visit last year they had again shrunk
two and one-half inches. How can they become shorter and
shorter? Does this not make us disappointed? If I were to go
next year and find that my small grandson is shorter than he
is this year, I would be disappointed and angry. I would not
dare to throw him out, but I would surely not be happy.
However, if I go next year and see that he has grown at least
five inches, as his grandfather I would be very happy and
want to come again and again.

Therefore, do not think that we have only Ephesians 1:23:
"[The church] is His Body, the fullness of the One who fills all
in all." You still must go on until you come to 4:13: "Until we
all arrive...at a full-grown man, at the measure of the stature
of the fullness of Christ." We must grow. How do we grow?
We grow by putting off the old man and putting on the new
man. That is to say, we grow by putting aside our natural
man. Instead of living by our natural man, we live by Christ
and in the spirit. This is the way we grow. Every day we
put off our natural being and live in the spirit. There is no
natural person here; only Christ is here. We are all one in
Christ. What the Lord wants today is not only the churches
on the ground of locality—one locality, one church—but also
the Body as His fullness. What the Lord wants today is the
Body, the fullness.

CHAPTER FOUR

THE BODY OF CHRIST
BEING THE FULLNESS OF CHRIST

Scripture Reading: Eph. 1:23; 4:10, 13; 1 Cor. 12:12

THE MEANING OF FULLNESS

We must pay attention to the fact that in the New Testament *fullness* is not an adjective but a noun. In the Chinese Union Version John 1:16 says, "For of His full grace we have all received." However, if you study this verse carefully, you will see that the word *grace* is not in the original Greek text. The proper translation of this clause is, "For of His fullness we have all received." Thus, according to the usage of the New Testament, *fullness* is not an adjective but a noun. The church is the Body of Christ. *Body* is a noun; the Body is His fullness, so *fullness* is also a noun. I hope that you would never consider fullness as an adjective. In the New Testament *fullness* is a noun just as *riches* is. For example, in Ephesians 3:16, which says, "According to His rich glory" (Chinese Union Version), the original text actually says, "According to the riches of His glory," both *riches* and *glory* being nouns. In our experience both *riches* and *fullness* are nouns. We enjoy the riches of Christ, and the result is that we are constituted to be the fullness of Christ. Then Ephesians 4:13 says that we must arrive at the measure of the stature of the fullness of Christ. In the book of Ephesians, *fullness* as a noun is used twice: His fullness (1:23) and the measure of the stature of the fullness of Christ (4:13).

The riches are outside of us and are objective, not yet having passed through our enjoyment and experience. The fullness is within us and is subjective, being the result of what we have enjoyed and experienced of the riches. If the riches of Christ are placed outside of us, they will be merely the riches of Christ and will not constitute the fullness of Christ. In order for His riches to be constituted into the fullness of Christ, they must be enjoyed, experienced, and digested by us and thus be constituted into the element of our entire being.

This fullness, which is the Body of Christ, has a stature. Because the fullness is the Body, it certainly has its stature, which in turn has its measure, which is the measure of the stature. I hope that everyone will remember this phrase in Ephesians 4:13: "the measure of the stature of the fullness of Christ." There are four nouns here—"measure," "stature," "fullness," and "Christ"—joined into one great phrase by three "ofs." Simply put, this is the measure of the stature of the fullness of Christ. But if we are not careful, we may easily understand *fullness* to be an adjective. Therefore, we must be trained that when we speak of the measure of the stature of the fullness of Christ, we do not mean *fullness* as an adjective but as a noun. If you were to understand *fullness* to be an adjective, you could easily change *fullness* into *full* and say "the full measure of the stature of Christ." This is completely wrong.

You may have this kind of understanding because you do not have the vision of the Body of Christ being the fullness of Christ. Not to mention Christians in general, even among us there are very few brothers and sisters who have a deep impression and a clear knowledge of the fullness of Christ, which is a marvelous matter. If you see this vision, you will never use *fullness* as an adjective. The fullness of Christ is a concrete item, but on the other hand, it is also spiritual, mysterious, and abstract. If I say that the church is the assembly of the called-out ones, you would not understand *assembly* as an adjective; but when I speak of the measure of the stature of the fullness of Christ, you may easily change *fullness* into an adjective in your usage. Why is this? It is because the assembly of the called-out ones is physical and easily seen by everyone; therefore, it is easy to understand. If, however, I say that the Body of Christ is the fullness of

Christ, this fullness is abstract. From God's view, from the spiritual view, the fullness is concrete; but from the physical view, it cannot be seen by human eyes, so it is abstract, and it is difficult for people to see this vision.

More than ten years ago, some among us proclaimed "the full Christ" and thought that they had seen the vision. However, this term is not in the Bible, and this is an erroneous understanding. In the New Testament the fullness is the issue of the overflow of Christ out of those who experience and enjoy Him. If you enjoy Christ and experience Him, and if I enjoy Christ and experience Him, then we will be full of Christ inwardly, and this Christ who fills us is His fullness.

CHRIST BEING THE HEAD
AND CHRIST BEING THE BODY

How then does Christ constitute Himself into us to become His fullness? I can say it in this way: The Lord Jesus in Himself is the Head, and the Lord Jesus constituted into us is the Body. A person is not a head only but a head with a body. If today I am here as a head hanging in the air and speaking to you, I believe you would be scared to death. If there were only a head without a body, this would not be a complete person. A complete person has both a head and a body. In the New Testament, the Lord Jesus in Himself is the Head, but when He gets into all of us and is constituted into us, then He is the Body. Thus, not only is the Head Christ, but also the Body is Christ. First Corinthians 12:12 says, "For even as the body is one and has many members, yet all the members of the body, being many, are one body, so also is the Christ." This verse clearly tells us that the Body is Christ. The Lord Jesus is the Head, and He is also the Body. We cannot say, however, that we are the Body and also the Head. We can be only the Body and cannot be the Head, but the Lord Jesus can be both the Head and the Body. In Himself, He is the Head, and in us collectively, He is the Body. The Head is individual, while the Body is corporate. Both are Christ.

Do not think, however, that because you are a Christian, someone else is a Christian, and I am a Christian, when we all come together, we are Christ. You should never say this, because there are certain conditions that must be met. When we all come together, we may be Christ or we may be completely Adam. Therefore, we should never think that simply because we are Christians, when we come together, we are Christ and that although we are many, we are one Body, and so also is the Christ. Perhaps when we first began to meet, there was a little bit of Christ, but once we begin to argue, we are void of Christ and become a gathering of old Adams.

Now do we all see what the church is? To say it more accurately, the church is Christ coming out of our experience of Him. Christianity is not the church, and even we in the Lord's recovery are not the church unless Christ comes out when we meet. The real church is Christ coming out from within His believers in their experience of Him. You enjoy Christ, I enjoy Christ, and we all enjoy Christ. You experience Christ, I experience Christ, and we all experience Christ. Then each time we come together, Christ flows out from our experiences. This is the church, the Body, which is the fullness of Christ. Christianity is not the Body of Christ, and neither is any group of Christians who merely meet together without allowing Christ to be lived out of them. Even we who are in the Lord's recovery meeting in the Lord's name are not the Body if we do not allow Christ to live out of us. The church is Christ lived out of the believers and experienced from within the believers.

You may ask me, "What about the ground of the church for oneness?" No one who allows Christ to be experienced from within would be divided from others, because Christ is definitely not divided. One who truly experiences Christ from within will certainly practice one church in each locality, and he will stand firm on the ground. This is because Christ is not divided; any division is not Christ. Spiritual matters are a wonder in that very often a little difference may result in a huge discrepancy. This is "to be off by a hair at the beginning and miss by a mile at the end." You should never think, "Isn't Brother So-and-so very spiritual? Isn't Brother So-and-so very deep in the Lord?" Yes, but even those who are deep can be divisive. Once you are in a division, you are no longer Christ; once you are divided, you are no longer in the Spirit, because there is no division in the Spirit. Do not worry about the matter of the ground; if a person allows Christ to be truly experienced from within, he will certainly be in the oneness.

THE BODY NEEDING TO GROW UNTIL IT ARRIVES AT THE PROPER MEASURE OF ITS STATURE

I repeat, the fullness is the Body of Christ. A body has a stature, and a stature has its measure; this body needs to grow. It is quite possible that as we are meeting here at this time, Christ is being experienced from within us, and this Christ experienced from within is the Body of Christ. However, please listen; the measure of the stature of the Body here is still not very large, so the Body needs to grow. Ephesians 4:13 says, "Until we all arrive at the oneness of the faith and of the full knowledge of the Son of God, at a full-grown man, at the measure of the stature of the fullness of Christ." The church in Taipei is the Body of Christ, but has this Body grown and arrived at the measure of the stature? This is still a question. Thus, we still must grow. Thank the Lord that today in all the local churches in the Lord's recovery, there is a small amount of the fullness of Christ, but the measure of the stature of the fullness is still in question, so there is the need for growth. Furthermore, this growth is not a matter of the increase in knowledge or doctrine; it is a matter of the daily increase in the experience and enjoyment of Christ. If, as the churches in all the localities, you enjoy more of Christ, experience more of Christ, have more Christ constituted into you, and have more Christ experienced from within you day by day, you will cause the measure of the stature of the fullness of Christ to increase in all the localities. This is not something that can happen in a year or so; rather, it is a matter of growing continually until we arrive at the measure of the stature which the fullness of Christ should have.

THE WAY TO GROW BEING BY ENJOYING THE PNEUMATIC LORD

How can we grow? There is only one way for you to grow, and there is only one way for the local churches to grow, and that is by enjoying the Lord. Brothers and sisters, we must clearly see that the Lord we enjoy today is not biblical knowledge or doctrine, nor is He a religious form or ordinance; He is none of these. The Lord whom we enjoy today is the Triune God, who was incarnated and who passed through death, resurrection, and ascension to become the all-inclusive, omnipresent Spirit. The Lord whom we experience is just this Spirit.

Looking at Matthew 3, Christianity says that the Holy Father, the Holy Son, and the Holy Spirit are three separate Persons: the Holy Father is an old man, the Holy Son is a younger man, and the Holy Spirit is a dove. This is the shallow view of many. They are constricted to Matthew 3 on this matter and do not have the knowledge of the entire Bible, which has many more chapters than simply Matthew 3. For example in John 14, Philip said to the Lord, "Lord, show us the Father and it is sufficient for us" (v. 8). The Lord Jesus then said, "Have I been so long a time with you, and you have not known Me, Philip? He who has seen Me has seen the Father; how is it that you say, Show us the Father?" (v. 9). Then in verses 16 through 20, the Lord said, "I will ask the Father, and He will give you another Comforter, that He may be with you forever....I will not leave you as orphans; I am coming to you....In that day you will know that I am in My Father, and you in Me, and I in you." Furthermore, 1 Corinthians 15:45b says, "The last Adam became a life-giving Spirit," and 2 Corinthians 3:17 says, "The Lord is the Spirit." Eventually, in Revelation, the last book of the Bible, there are seven epistles written to seven churches. At the beginning of each epistle is a description of the Lord Jesus as the One who speaks to the churches, but at the end of each these epistles it says that it is the Spirit who speaks to the churches. This proves that the Lord Jesus who speaks at the beginning of the epistles is the Spirit who speaks at the end. These passages in the New Testament reveal to us that the Father, the Son, and the Spirit are one God.

Our God is the unique God; this God became flesh, died on the cross for the redemption of our sins, and resurrected with His humanity completely uplifted and mingled with His divinity. Today He is an all-inclusive, life-giving Spirit. We must clearly see that today He is such a Spirit. We should constantly open ourselves to Him as such a Spirit through His precious blood. From our experience we know that when we open our spirit to Him, we can touch Him. This is to contact the Spirit by our spirit, fellowship with the Spirit by our spirit, and respond to the Spirit by our spirit. This is what is referred to in 1 Corinthians 6:17: "But he who is joined to the Lord is one spirit." This is truly glorious! Every day by the precious blood we can open our spirit to contact the Lord as the Spirit. In such a contact we breathe Him in, eat Him, drink Him, and enjoy Him so that in our daily life He can saturate every part of our being—our emotion, our mind and thoughts, and our will. When this happens, we do not live by ourselves, but we live by the Lord who has saturated our entire being. What is this? This is Christ experienced out of us, and this Christ who is experienced out of us is the Body, which is the fullness.

The fullness involves a measure. Our measure today is not enough, so we need to enjoy and experience Him every day. When we enjoy Him and experience Him every day, the measure of the stature gradually increases until one day we will arrive at the measure of the stature of the fullness. Praying, reading the Word, meeting, and coming together to read the life-studies all help in this matter, but it is not these things that cause us to grow. Rather, it is the life-giving Spirit—Christ Himself—who causes us to grow. When we pray, we must touch Him; when we read the Word, we must touch Him; when we read the life-studies, we must touch Him— Christ as the living Spirit. It is not a matter of your coming to read human words, nor is it even a matter of your coming to read the black and white letters of the Bible. Rather, it is a matter of your inwardly touching the Lord and being supplied in spirit through reading the Word, praying, and reading the life-study messages. It is not to have more doctrines; it is to be fed inwardly and to have more life in your spirit. This is to grow to the stature of the fullness of Christ.

The brothers have told me that because in all the localities the brothers and sisters enjoy the life-study messages, many of them have been inwardly supplied, have been nourished, and have experienced the inner growth of life. In this visit I also have certainly sensed a difference here. This shows that it is not a matter of doctrines, knowledge, or outwardly reading the Word and praying, but it is a matter of truly touching the Lord inwardly.

Do not forget, however, that as soon as we touch the Lord inwardly, the Lord begins to operate in us. In the Bible this operation is called transformation. Once He begins to operate, we are being inwardly transformed. This transformation is organic and metabolic. If you make up your mind and decide to change yourself, I would tell you not to believe in your change. Your decision is not trustworthy, because the Bible says, "To will is present with me, but to work out the good is not" (Rom. 7:18). Romans 8 says that we should walk according to the spirit. It is not a matter of willing to do good, but a matter of walking according to the spirit. How do you walk according to the spirit? You do not need to study; you just need to open yourself up to read the Word, to pray, and to fellowship together with others about the life-study messages. Then you will touch Christ inwardly, and He will enter into you to saturate every part of your being. Thus, you will unconsciously be transformed and will spontaneously live out a condition that you might not even be aware of, but others will say that you have really changed. If you were to set your will to do this, you might succeed for three and a half days or even for a week, but when you succeed, you will be proud of your accomplishment and will feel that you are not so bad. However, when Christ nourishes and transforms you within, you will not feel it. To you, it will be something spontaneous, but others will sense that you have changed. This is the increase of Christ within you.

The increase of Christ within you is not an objective matter. If we add water to an empty bottle, that is objective. But the increase of Christ is the issue of an organic, metabolic transformation. Therefore, the Bible illustrates our experience and enjoyment of Christ as eating Christ. In John 6 the Lord says that He is edible and that he who eats Him shall live because of Him (v. 57). We all know that whatever food we take into us causes an organic function within us, which is called metabolism. The food that you eat is digested and absorbed into your cells to become you. This is not an objective addition, but a subjective growth. In other words, you eat Christ and eventually you become Christ. This is why Paul could say, "For to me, to live is Christ" (Phil. 1:21a).

THE WORDS OF THE OPPOSERS
BEING MERELY SLANDER

Some people in Christianity do not have this light. In the past year or two in the United States, some opposers wrote pamphlets against us, saying that we teach evolution, that man can evolve into God. Do you think this is right? On the one hand, Paul certainly did say, "For to me, to live is Christ"; in this sense Paul had become Christ. First Timothy 3:16 also says that the church is God manifested in the flesh. However, the opposers are saying that we make ourselves part of the Godhead as the object of man's worship. Some even say that the people in the local churches teach this to such an extent that eventually they have made themselves God, and therefore they themselves are the object of worship in their meetings, even to worship themselves in their meetings.

In this training at this time, however, we have to learn to speak the word of the truth. We worship God in His Godhead; we do not worship those who have His divine nature. We can be transformed into the image of God (2 Cor. 3:18), having the divine nature (2 Pet. 1:4), but we absolutely cannot become the Person of God or the Godhead. We can never share the Godhead. The opposers say that in our teaching we say that we can become the Godhead; this is slander. We are not transformed to be a part of the Godhead; rather, we are transformed to have the divine nature. Today we do have God's divine nature within us, but we cannot share His Godhead. The Godhead is special and unique, but because of the divine life, we may have the divine nature in a general, or universal, way. As I have said, Christ is the Head and the Body, but we are the Body and cannot be the Head; the Head is a matter related to the Godhead.

Some opposers also say that we teach pantheism. Because we teach that Christ is all and Christ is everything, they say that we make everything Christ, even making the tables and chairs Christ. We ourselves also must be careful. Do not think that because we say Christ is the One who fills all in all that we are saying that all the animals and all the physical things contain Christ. This is the speaking of those who slander us. Such slanderous words contain and are involved with the mysteries and deep things of Satan (Rev. 2:24). Even though the devil is disturbing us, I would like to assure you that the messages we have released are all pure and that they are based upon the divine speaking in the Bible and upon our experience. We do not teach that man can evolve into God, and neither do we teach pantheism. We teach that the unique Creator, who is the Triune God, became flesh and shed His blood to accomplish redemption. Then He rose from the dead and brought His humanity into resurrection, uplifting His humanity and mingling it with divinity. Now He is the all-inclusive, all-accomplishing, life-giving Spirit. He is here waiting for people to believe into Him, receive Him, and enjoy Him. We, the redeemed sinners, must constantly open to Him by His blood to absorb the supply of this all-inclusive Spirit. He frequently contacts us, touches us, and supplies us. As we enjoy Him, He becomes our experience; He spreads out from our spirit, saturating every part of our being until we are filled with Him. In a sense, we have become Him in life and in nature but not in the Godhead. We can say, "For to me, to live is Christ," and when we come together it is the manifestation of God in the flesh. This is based entirely upon the Bible and can be confirmed by our experience. I believe that now these words can make us clearer about what the church is, how the church is the Body, how the church is the fullness, how this fullness also has a stature with its measure, and how the measure of this stature still needs to grow.

I most surely believe that the voices of the opposers may spread throughout the entire earth. If you young ones are not clear, when you hear their speaking, you will not be able to discern what is true and what is false. This is why I want to make it clear from the outset. You must know that their words are slanderous. You must know that we can never become the Godhead, but we can partake of the divine nature.

Second Peter 1:4 says, "Through which He has granted to us precious and exceedingly great promises that through these you might become partakers of the divine nature." We are partakers of the divine nature because we are the children born of God. Every child has the life and the nature of his father, but this does not mean that the child eventually will become his father. We have God's life and God's nature, but this does not mean that we will become the Godhead. Nor do we say that Christ fills all, and He fills you and me, and therefore we make all things God, which is pantheism. We acknowledge that Christ fills all, that today He is in the heavens and on the earth, that even now He is in this meeting place and within us; He certainly fills all of us. However, this is not pantheism.

BEING DELIVERED FROM RELIGIOUS RITUALS, PAYING ATTENTION ONLY TO THE ONENESS OF THE FAITH

In addition, there is another problem, that is, so-called religious piety. We may illustrate what religious piety is by the following example. Some people are not satisfied with the present condition of our meetings because we shout, pray loudly, and release our spirits. From their youth they have been taught that they must be careful with the way they walk when they enter a "sanctuary." They must walk as slowly and as quietly as possible. When I was young and was meeting with the Brethren, I was taught the same thing. Whenever we met together, we were so quiet that you could hear a pin drop. But that kind of silence is the silence of the tomb. Only a cemetery is this quiet and orderly. If you go to a kindergarten, however, you will see little children hopping and jumping with much noise. I would rather have a noisy, bustling kindergarten than a quiet, orderly cemetery. Others criticize our meetings because it seems that there is no beginning and no end. Most Christian worship services on Sunday mornings have a set format; they begin with a hymn and end with a benediction. But when you come to our meetings, a small sister in the corner next to the wall may say, "O Lord, hallelujah, amen!" and the meeting begins. We do not have preachers or pastors; sometimes everybody speaks in our meetings, and there is no benediction at the end. I would like to tell you, however, that there is no need to pay attention to these matters. If you pay attention to these things, immediately you will be far from the oneness of the faith.

I can never forget the summer of 1932, when Brother Nee was invited to speak to the graduating class of a seminary in Huang County, Shantung Province, and I took a special leave of absence from work to accompany him. That was the first time I had ever been in a meeting of the Pentecostal movement. When I went in, I saw some of them rolling, some jumping, some laughing, and some saying, "I have seen a vision, a great, great light!" They called those things "holy rolling," "holy jumping," and "holy laughter." There were several hundred people in the hall, but everyone was acting in his own way for quite a long time. Brother Nee could not speak the message until they were finished. Later the pastor told everyone to stop, and finally he picked up a bell to ring. Still, no one paid attention to him; everyone kept acting in his own way. It was the first time I had seen such a situation, and I could not bear it or take it. After the pastor had rung the bell for a very long time, everybody finally stopped, and then Brother Nee spoke a message.

After Brother Nee had spoken and left the platform, I accompanied him for a walk on the school campus. I said, "Brother Nee, I cannot take their meetings with the rolling and laughing and jumping." I thought Brother Nee would think the same way I did. However, he did not say whether he approved or disapproved. He simply said in a light, moderate tone, "There is no word in the New Testament that tells us definitely what is the right way to meet." When I heard this, I thought that Brother Nee approved of their way. Later I learned that he did not necessarily approve of their situation. Nevertheless, because at that time he had a very clear vision and very clear light, when he listened to what I was saying, he knew that I was still in religious rituals. He was very wise, however, and did not rebuke me; he said only in a gentle manner that the New Testament does not definitely tell us how to meet. He said this to deliver me from religious rituals.

If we truly know and experience the Son of God and truly become His Body, His fullness, we will not care for forms of meeting. This is why from the beginning we have paid absolutely no attention to any regulations, especially in the beginning of the testimony in America. In 1960 before I went to America, I spoke many messages in Taipei, hoping that you all could be delivered from rituals. I spoke over a period of about a year, but the more I spoke, the more you became dead; the more I spoke, the more you stopped moving. Therefore, when the Lord took me to America, because of the lessons I had learned in the Far East, right from the beginning I did not set up any forms among them. This is the Lord's great deliverance. I hope that today even our calling on the Lord's name, our pray-reading, our pray-singing, and everything we do will not become our forms. It is even possible that our meeting tomorrow will be very quiet yet still be full of the Spirit and life. We must not have any rituals.

My main point is this: You must see Ephesians 4:13, which says, "Until we all arrive at the oneness of the faith." It is not the oneness of any doctrine, but the oneness of the faith. Whether shouting or whispering, whether being noisy or being quiet, these things are not important because they are not matters related to the faith. Our faith is the Lord Jesus Himself, including His Person and His work. As we continue to grow in Christ until the day we become full-grown, we should put away all these differences, which are like toys. We should pay attention only to our faith, which is the Person and work of Christ.

I speak these things lest you be bothered by some practices. We must see very clearly that the church is the Body of Christ, and this Body is the fullness of Christ, and this fullness must grow up gradually. By our contacting Him more, receiving Him more, enjoying Him more, and experiencing Him more, He will be constituted more in our entire being and experienced out from our entire being. This is the true church, the practical church. His fullness is His Body; thus, we can say that it is just Christ. The Lord in Himself is the Head, and the Lord in all of us is this one Body.

CHAPTER FIVE

THE NEW MAN BEING UNIQUELY ONE

Scripture Reading: Eph. 2:15-16; 4:3, 22, 24; Rom. 15:6; 1 Cor. 1:10

TOUCHING THE DEEPEST MATTERS

In these messages, we can say that we are touching some of the deepest matters in the New Testament, and we can say that these are matters that Christianity has not touched for centuries. The church is the Body of Christ. The term *Body* has been used many times in the writings of Christianity, but the writers have not touched the particular points concerning the Body, nor have they seen the vision of the Body. We thank the Lord that over these past years God has clearly revealed this vision to us from His Word. However, those of us who are to receive this vision need a preparation or condition beforehand. In previous years we did not see that there was this condition and preparation needed. Now in this training, however, I feel that there is the right kind of condition; therefore, this is the time for these messages to be released.

The vision, the revelation, concerning the Body is very deep. Therefore, when we speak of it, we must speak very accurately. It is true that the Body is the church, but this is not an objective matter. The Body is the riches of Christ constituted into us to make us the fullness of Christ. The riches of Christ are what Christ is to us. It is not that the fullness of Christ is what Christ is to us; rather, the fullness of Christ is what we are to Christ. Christ is our riches, and we are Christ's fullness. To us, Christ is the riches; to Christ, we are the fullness. This fullness, however, is not constituted by ourselves or with ourselves. It is true that the fullness is what we are to Christ, but this fullness is constituted with the element of Christ; that is, it is the riches of Christ worked into us that constitute or make us His fullness. Therefore, when you touch this matter, you must be very accurate in your speaking.

THE NEW MAN BEING UNIQUELY ONE

At this time we must go on to see that the Body of Christ is for the new man in the New Testament. In the New Testament there is a new man. From my youth I was taught in Christianity to know that before we were saved, we had an old man, and that after we are saved, we have a new man; every saved person has a new man, so there are many new men. For the past twenty or thirty years this impression has been with me. However, one day the Lord opened my eyes and showed me through the book of Ephesians that the new man is not plural. Rather, the new man is uniquely one. There is only one new man in the universe.

Ephesians 2:15 says, "Abolishing in His flesh the law of the commandments in ordinances, that He might create the two in Himself into one new man." There are ordinances in the law, and these ordinances are a barrier between people. When Christ was on the cross, not only did He take away our sins, crucify our old man, and destroy the devil, but He also abolished the ordinances. On the cross, when Christ removed the barriers between people by abolishing the ordinances, He created the two, the Jewish believers and the Gentile believers, in Himself into one new man. I certainly saw a vision in this verse. I saw that today there are not many new men; rather, there is only one new man. We are not individually new men; instead, you are a part of the new man, I am a part of the new man, and all the saved ones are also parts of the new man. The new man is uniquely one, yet this new man has millions of parts. There is only one Body, and there is only one new man—one Body and one new man. Ephesians 2:15 says, "That He might create the two in Himself into one new man." This is sufficient proof that the new man is corporate, not individual.

Then verse 16 says, "And might reconcile both in one Body to God through the cross, having slain the enmity by it." The creation of the one new man is in verse 15, and the one Body is in verse 16. This shows us that the one new man in the former verse is the one Body in the latter verse, and it also shows us that the Body and the new man are absolutely related.

THE BODY BEING A MATTER OF LIFE
AND THE NEW MAN BEING A MATTER OF PERSON

The Bible has a few passages that are so profound that our natural mind cannot understand them at all. Why is the one new man also the one Body? Why does verse 15 say that Christ has created the two in Himself into one new man, while verse 16 says that He has reconciled both in one Body to God? There must be a reason and an explanation for this. What then is the difference between the Body and the new man?

First, we must see that the Body is a matter of life, and the new man is a matter of person. Our body has life in it; without life, it is not a body but a corpse. When we speak of the Body, we understand that it has life in it. Thus, the Body is a matter of life. When we speak of one new man, though, it is a matter of person. A man has a person. Today my body does not need a person; my body only needs life. In other words, my body needs to be healthy, and health is life. When I have a rich and proper life within me, my body is healthy. If my life has a problem, my body becomes sick. Therefore, the body is a matter of life. The new man, however, is a matter of person. My body cannot plan where it will go, but my person can make a plan. There is a person within me who decides, saying, "This morning this body will go to this place, and this evening this body will go to that place." By this you can see the difference between the person and the life that is in the body. The person makes a decision about where to go, and the body immediately takes action. The Body of Christ is a matter of life, whereas the new man is a matter of person.

Still, you all must know that both the life and the person are Christ. The life in this Body is Christ, and the person in this one new man is also Christ. The church is the Body, and this Body needs Christ to be in it as life. The church is also the one new man, and this one new man needs Christ to be in him as his person.

IN THE BODY WE BEING MEMBERS ONE OF ANOTHER

As I have said before, Christianity teaches people mostly to love one another, and if you cannot love, you must simply give up. However, the New Testament tells us not only to love one another but also to be members one of another. Being members one of another is not something you can give up. In our body the hand is beneath the arm, and the arm is beneath the shoulder; regardless of whether or not they love one another, they are members one of another. You must see this vision. I speak truthfully that it is this vision that has bound me for forty-five years. You should never think that all the brothers who coordinate with me in the service, whether co-workers, elders, older ones, or younger ones, are according to my taste. I would like to tell you that out of ten brothers eight and a half are not according to my taste, and the remaining one and a half are only twenty percent according to my taste and eighty percent not according to my taste. When you calculate all this, you can see there is not much that is according to our taste. What then should we do?

This is why in the past I made the following calculations again and again to determine the gains and losses involved. First, I calculated whether or not I wanted to be a man. This, however, was not something for me to decide; it was God's ordination. Since God ordained me to be a man, there was no way for me to avoid it. Likewise, in your case God also ordained that you would be a man. Please forgive me for saying that I sometimes cannot understand why I had to be born. If I had not been born, then I would not have so many troubles. Nevertheless, this was something not up to me; I was simply born. Should I, then, be a man or not? I should.

Then I went on to calculate. Since I am a man, should I be a Christian? There is no way not to be. If I am a man but not a Christian, then it is truly, "Woe is me, for I am finished!"

Therefore, I have to be a Christian because there is no other way.

Next, I considered that since I am a Christian, should I be a Christian in the denominations? I should not. Then what should I do? I should do things according to the Bible. After all these considerations—from the first question to the second, to the third, and to the fourth—I eventually became completely chained and shackled. Since according to the Bible I must be a Christian, what does the Bible say about a Christian? The Bible tells me that since I am a Christian, a member of the Body, I cannot be without others. Therefore, at times I could only go to the Lord and complain secretly to Him, saying, "Lord, this brother is not very good. Why did You put me together with him?" I knew that if I complained too much, the Lord may say, "All right, since you don't like this one, I will give you another one." I knew what would happen next. Although the taste of the coordination at the time was very hot, if I went on to complain to the Lord, He may give me something even hotter. Therefore, after complaining, I immediately confessed my sins. Do you agree with what I have said? I do know this matter.

I am already more than seventy years old, and I have tasted many bitter, hot, sour, and sweet things. I certainly have some knowledge of the Lord, and I know His ways; therefore, I tell you that you should never complain. Once you complain, it will be heat upon heat. The next one you get will be even harder for you to bear. The heat will reach a point where you will not be able even to feel it anymore. At this point in your situation, hot or not hot is all the same, so you stop your complaining. When you get to this stage, you are about ready to graduate.

Thus, the conclusions of my calculations were: I have no choice but to be a man; as a man, I must be a Christian; and as a Christian, I must be a member of the Body. As to the brothers and sisters who are my co-workers and my fellow members, it was not I who sought them out. I did not seek them out; it was the Lord who sent them to me, one by one. While one brother moves as fast as lightning, another brother is exactly the opposite. When you explain something to this slow one, you can speak for three days and three nights, and he still will not understand. Nevertheless, since he is a fellow member, I cannot expel him. An employer can discharge an employee, but the arm cannot expel the hand. If the arm were to expel the hand, the hand may not suffer, but without the hand, the arm would not be able to do anything.

Today we see that Christianity does not have the Body; instead, everyone simply comes together. If today they are happy, they will come together; if tomorrow they are unhappy, they will just forget about it. In the Lord's economy, however, if you have really seen the Lord's Body and that the brothers and sisters are members one of another, that is enough. There is nothing to discuss; you are simply a member, and you have no choice but to be a member. If you merely love one another, then when you are happy, you love the others, and when you are unhappy, you do not love them. However, as a member, you have no choice but to be a member; whether or not you are happy, you are a member.

IN THE NEW MAN THERE BEING ONLY ONE MOUTH

The Body is a matter of being members one of another, but for the new man the requirements are even more than what the Body requires. For many years I read Romans 15:6, which says, "That with one accord you may with one mouth glorify... God." I felt that I did not understand this word. How could so many Christians come together and have only one mouth? I did not understand it at that time. One day, however, I saw that the church is one new man. How many mouths does a man have? It has one. Not only are we all members one of another, but we also all speak with one mouth. Do you see how much is required of us? It is already restricting enough to be members one of another, and now even when we speak, we all have to have one mouth. This is not my word; it is Paul's word. How many mouths does the one new man have? One. Then who is the mouth? If you say that Christ is the mouth, you are too transcendent. In order to resolve this matter you must see that there is only one new man with only one person. In the whole body there is only one mouth, but who controls this mouth? It is the person who controls the mouth.

The church is not merely the Body but also the one new man. The Body needs Christ as its life, whereas the new man needs Christ as his person. When you want to speak, when I want to speak, when any one of us wants to speak, we must resolve the basic question: Who is the person that is speaking here? If you are the person, you have your own mouth. If I am the person, I have my own mouth. Thus, you have your mouth, and I have my mouth; therefore, there are two mouths. When each one is a person individually and each one speaks his own matters, we have many mouths. This is a society or a denomination, and this is the condition of today's degraded Christianity. In the Lord's recovery, however, the church is the Body, and the church is the one new man. The Body has Christ as life, and the new man has Christ as a person. When you speak, it is not you who are the person; when I speak, neither is it I. When anyone speaks, it is Christ who is the person. What is the result? The result is that there is only one mouth.

This is why in 1 Corinthians 1:10 Paul says that all "speak the same thing." This verse greatly bothered me many years ago. I thought, "How could all Christians speak the same thing?" It seemed to me that this was impossible, but one day I understood. The church is the one new man with only one person, and this person controls our speaking, so whatever He speaks is surely "the same thing" that we all speak as the new man.

Many preachers and pastors in today's Christianity are all their own persons, all have their own mouths, and all speak their own things. Therefore, they have many mouths, each speaking a different thing. However, the church is not like this. The church is the one new man with Christ as her person. Whenever the brothers and sisters are about to speak something, they do not take themselves as the person; instead, they allow Christ to be the person. You let Christ be your person when you speak, and I let Christ be my person when I speak. Eventually, everyone speaks the same thing.

Consider the Bible. The Old and New Testaments contain

sixty-six books written by more than forty different authors in many different places over a period of fifteen or sixteen hundred years. The first book, Genesis, was written about 1500 B.C., while the last book, Revelation, was written after A.D. 90. Do they all have one mouth? Do they all speak the same thing? The entire Bible has one mouth and speaks the same thing, even though it was written over a long period of time by many different people in many different places. Now you can understand what it means to have one mouth speaking the same thing. In the East, in the West, in the United States, in Germany, in Great Britain, in Japan, and in Korea, we can have many people speaking, but all have one mouth and say one thing. Although we are many and we come from many places, all of us have one mouth, and we all speak the same thing. This is because we all are the one new man having only one person.

Dear brothers and sisters, what I have fellowshipped with you here is something that I know. Many times I wanted to speak, but I checked within, asking myself, "Is it I who want to speak or is it the Lord?" In other words, in the matter of speaking, is the Lord the person, or am I the person? If it is I, there will be a problem; if it is the Lord, there will be no problem. If I allow the Lord to be the person, He is the One who speaks; then two months later, if you allow the Lord to be the person, you will speak the same thing that I have spoken. We have one mouth speaking the same thing.

In Christianity today you see a pitiful condition because every preacher wants to speak his own thing, and he thinks it is a shame to speak what others have spoken. Thus, you speak your thing and he speaks his; sometimes someone will use something from someone else's speaking, but he will do it secretly. This has actually happened in America. Fifteen years ago, before the Lord's recovery went to the United States, almost no one spoke about the "human spirit" and "transformation," but now these have become common terms. There are also some people who used our materials to study the book of Romans, and after they finished their studies and printed them, they said that they discovered these things themselves through their own study. This is not proper.

There is, however, another condition in which people blindly follow others: I speak whatever you speak, and you speak whatever I speak. In this way we make a show to everyone that we all have only one mouth and we speak the same thing. You must see that in neither case is the condition right. We do not want the condition in Christianity, nor do we want a condition of blindly following others. We want a condition in which the one new man speaks. There is only one new man, and this one new man has only one person, so the one new man speaks with one mouth and says the same thing.

THERE BEING NO FREEDOM
TO SPEAK OUR OWN THINGS IN THE NEW MAN

In the new man there is no freedom to speak your own things. This is more limiting and restricting than being members one of another. Everyone knows that what limits you the most is the matter of speaking. If I cannot say this or that—whatever I like—then I am very much restricted, but if I can say whatever I want, then I am very free. However, in the church, in the Body of Christ, and especially in the new man, neither your natural man nor my natural man has freedom of speech. This is because we ourselves are not the persons. In the one new man there is only one person. Only this person has the freedom to speak, and our natural man has absolutely no freedom of speech. The Lord has the absolute freedom to speak, and I absolutely have no freedom to speak. We cannot allow the natural man to speak; we definitely must not allow it. Only the one person should speak.

You have to consider "one mouth" in Romans 15:6 and "speak the same thing" in 1 Corinthians 1:10 together with "one new man" in Ephesians 2:15. Otherwise, you will never understand the first two verses. You may wonder how the entire church can have only one mouth and how millions of members can speak the same thing. Humanly speaking, this is absolutely impossible. However, we must see that in Romans 15, Paul was speaking of a local church. In a local church, there must be only one mouth. Here in Taipei, there should be only one mouth. There should also be only one mouth in the churches in Southeast Asia. This is because there is only one person. In the past you had too many mouths because you had too many persons. When there are many persons, there are many ideas; when there are many ideas, there are many opinions, but we thank the Lord that now there is one mouth and one person here. There are no policemen here; each of us is absolutely free, but on the other hand, you have absolutely no freedom because within you there is another person. You may be about to speak, but something "pinches" you from within, telling you not to say anything. All you can say is, "Thank the Lord!" When you want to speak again, the Lord pinches you again, so you simply say, "Amen!" If the Lord did not pinch this one and that one, I tell you, the brothers and sisters would most certainly quarrel when they come together.

There are many people in the church in Taipei, but there is no quarreling. The reason is that for many years they have had the grace to take Christ as their person. It is not I speaking, nor is it you speaking, nor is it he speaking, nor is it the brothers speaking, nor is it the sisters speaking; instead, everyone says, "Lord, You speak!"

Do not think that the reason we do not speak is because we were born with only half a lip. No, rather it seems that we were born with eight lips. Many years ago, however, when I was young, I made those careful calculations. It was not up to me to be a man, but if I am a man, then I must be a Christian; if I am going to be a Christian, then I must be one according to the Bible; if I am going to live according to the Bible, then I will be "chained." Hence, many times at critical moments I did not say anything. Why? Because the person within me did not speak. I am not the person; Christ is. We should take Christ not only to be our life but also to be our person. We should not only eat His riches to take them in and assimilate them into our being; we should also allow Him to be our person.

TOGETHER TAKING CHRIST AS THE PERSON IN THE NEW MAN

If you visit Christianity throughout all the world, you will

not hear the phrase "taking Christ as the person." This
matter, however, is truly in the Bible because the church is
the new man. Today this new man needs a person, and who
is this person? It is Christ Himself. How do we know this?
It is because Ephesians 3:17 says, "That Christ may make
His home in your hearts." If Christ wants to make His home
in our hearts, does this not mean that He wants to be the
person there? When you live in a house and make it your
home, then you become the person of that house. Ephesians
says more clearly than the other books that we must let
Christ make His home in our hearts, and this is because He
wants to be the person in us.

This, however, does not mean that He is in you as your
person, He is in me as my person, and He is in another one as
his person. This is an improper understanding. I tell you that
He is in all of us as one person. The person in you is the
person who is in me. We all have only one person. Who is this
person? This person is Christ.

Brothers and sisters, in the last days of this age, before the
Lord will be able to return, we must see the Body and the new
man. When we come to the end of the Bible, in Revelation 22,
the Spirit and the bride appear. At the end the new man is a
bride. The church's experience in Christ definitely must
arrive at this stage. First it is the Body, then it is the
new man, and finally it is the bride. It is not as some say in
Christianity, that the believers will be gathered into one
place, and the Lord will change them instantly into His bride.
Instead, today we must receive grace to see the Body, to see
the new man, and finally to see the bride.

THE BODY BEING FOR MOVING
AND THE NEW MAN BEING FOR LIVING

We still have not arrived at the highest point in our vision
because our knowledge of the Body is insufficient, our knowledge of the new man is not enough, and also our knowledge of
the bride is very limited. Nevertheless, I hope that we can see
something concerning the Body and the new man. The Body
is a matter of life, and the new man is a matter of person. The
Body is for moving; it is an instrument for action. Thus, it was

in one Body that the Lord Jesus reconciled both the Jewish and Gentile believers to God. This reconciliation is a Body matter. In the past we thought that when you were saved, you were reconciled to God, and when I was saved, I was reconciled to God. In other words, we thought that we were individually saved and individually reconciled to God. This is an erroneous concept. We must see that we who were far off and separated from God were reconciled to God not individually but in a corporate instrument. What is this instrument? This instrument is the Body of Christ. In one Body both the Jewish believers and the Gentile believers have been reconciled to God. This shows us that the Body is an instrument used by Christ.

When we move, we move in our body. For example, when I came downstairs today, I did it in my body. As I speak to you now, I am doing it in my body. If I were not in my body, there would be no way for me to speak. All my actions are in my body. My body is an instrument for different actions. When the church preaches the gospel, this is an action, and this action is in the Body and is carried out by the Body. Our body is an instrument for moving. Our life needs to increase and grow in order that our body might be healthy and strong enough to meet the need of our moving.

Then what about the new man? The new man is not for moving; the new man is for decision-making and for living. As a human being you may not move at all, but you still must live. The Body is for moving, and the new man is for living. Concerning the new man, Ephesians 4:24 says that it was created according to God in righteousness and holiness. Righteousness and holiness are conditions of our living. Thus, living is entirely a matter of the new man. The new man is for living, and eighty to ninety percent of our living is in making decisions. Therefore, you can see two things: the church as the Body is for moving, and the church as the new man is for living by making decisions. On the one hand, the church is the Body of Christ, and we take Christ as our life to act, to work, and to bear responsibilities. On the other hand, the church is the new man, and we take Christ as our person to make plans and to decide on how we should live. Whether it is the Body or the new man, whether in working and moving or in living and in deciding, everything is corporate; nothing is individual. You must see that your living today is the living of the new man, a corporate living, and your decisions are corporate decisions and not your personal decisions. For example, you may be trying to decide and to conclude whether you should open a factory or become an educator. There is a kind of living here. If you see that you are a part in the new man, you will not want to decide by yourself as the person. You will want to take Christ as your person together with all the other parts in the new man. At this time, when you are about to make a decision concerning your human life, you will not take yourself as the person; rather, you will take Christ as your person in the new man to make the decision. When you live your life by taking Christ as your person, your living will be the living of the new man.

The living of the new man has two characteristics: one is righteousness and the other is holiness. Righteousness is according to God's ways, and holiness is according to God's nature. When all the things in your living, whether great or small, are exactly the same in their nature as God's nature and exactly the same in their ways as God's ways, then there is holiness and righteousness. However, this kind of living is not the individual living of sanctification referred to in Christianity. Rather, the kind of living meant here is that you live a life in the new man by Christ as the person and that He is the One who makes all the decisions in you. Thus, whatever is lived out is righteousness and holiness. This is not related to our move or work; it is related only to our living. This is the aspect of the new man. The other aspect is the Body. As the Body, we move. Christ is our Head, so we move, and our moving is not based on our own strength or our own life but upon Christ as our life and strength. Furthermore, our move is not as individuals.

These two matters show that we cannot be individualistic. We must see that we are a corporate Body, and we are a corporate new man. Our living is corporate, and our moving is corporate. In our moving we take Christ as our life, and in our living we take Christ as our person. In the Body, Christ is our life, and in the new man, Christ is our person. In the Body we are members one of another, and in the new man we all have one mouth to speak the same thing. This is the church.

Chapter Six

PUTTING ON THE LIVING OF THE NEW MAN

Scripture Reading: Eph. 4:11-16

THE BODY AND THE NEW MAN
BEING THE HIGHEST VISION OF GOD

As we have said before, on the one hand, the church is the Body, and on the other hand, the church is the new man. In the Body we are members one of another, but in the new man what are we to one another? I cannot say for sure, but you must understand that in the new man all of us are simply one man. This requirement is as high as the heavens. Loving one another is a basic requirement, being members one of another is a requirement that is somewhat higher, but the requirement that everyone be only one man is exceedingly high. Consider this: If we were merely a group of people, it would be enough for us simply to love one another, yield to one another, be kind to one another, and take care of one another. But if we are a Body, loving one another is not enough; we must also be members one of another. Today, however, we are not only one Body but also one new man.

God has an eternal purpose, which is to obtain the church. To the Father, the church is His house; to Christ, the church is His Body; with respect to God's move in the universe, the church is a new man. It is very pitiful, however, that Christianity has never presented this to people. All that Christianity has presented is a religion with an object of worship and a set of related teachings to make people revere and worship God and to teach people according to their worship. This is too far off from God's purpose. If it is religion that God wants, then the Chinese culture would be good enough. What God wants, however, far surpasses religion. What God wants is the church that is composed of regenerated persons. These regenerated ones are also reconstituted ones, or according to the biblical expression, transformed ones. The purpose of regeneration, reconstitution, and transformation is that we may become the church. This church is the Body of Christ that moves on the earth, and this church is also the new man who lives out God's economy on the earth. This is something missing in Christianity today. We thank God that in these days He has opened up His Word to us.

Over the past few years, God has repeatedly shown us this matter. I can say that I have been waiting for an opportunity to speak about this matter because it is very deep and very high, and it is beyond what we can imagine. This matter is the church as the Body of Christ to be His fullness and concerning the church as the new man. In the Body, Christ is our life; in the new man, Christ is our person. Our moving is according to the Body with Christ as our inward life, and our living is according to the new man with Christ in it as our person.

In this training I hope that you will learn to speak accurately about the Body, the fullness, and the new man. I also hope that you will learn to speak the high things. Here there is no male or female. We know what it is that we are speaking. The church is the Body of Christ, and this is the fullness of Christ. In this fullness there is only Christ; there are no brothers and no sisters. In this new man there are not even any members because members are a matter of the Body, not a matter of the new man. The new man is not about members; the new man is about the person. Who is your person? Is it you or is it the Lord Jesus? The Lord Jesus is your person.

THE BODY AND THE NEW MAN BEING RELATED

In this message we must go on to see that in Ephesians, when the apostle Paul was writing this Epistle, within him he could not forget these two things: the Body and the new man. At the end of chapter one he referred to the church as His Body, the fullness of the One who fills all in all. Then in chapter two he said that Christ had slain the enmity between the Jews and Gentiles and created the two in Himself into one new man. Then he went on to say that through the cross both were reconciled to God in one Body. Therefore, you can see that the apostle always spoke of the Body and the new man together. When he mentioned the one, he could not forget the other; when he spoke about the other, he had to speak also about the one. Hence, it is always the Body and the new man.

The clearest example of this is in 4:13 where the apostle Paul put the two into one verse, saying, "Until we all arrive at the oneness of the faith and of the full knowledge of the Son of God, at a full-grown man." This full-grown man refers to the new man that has become full-grown. Then he said, "At the measure of the stature of the fullness of Christ." Therefore, you can see that at the end of 4:13, Paul in his speaking put the Body and the new man together, but this time he first mentioned the new man and then the Body. The new man here is a full-grown man, and the Body here is the measure of the stature of the fullness of Christ.

Here we must continue to speak about these two things: the Body and the new man. It is hard for us to say which should be first and which is second. In some places we see that we need the new man first, and in other places we see that we need the Body first.

PERFECTING THE SAINTS TO EXERCISE THEIR OWN FUNCTION

If we want to understand Ephesians 4:13, we must begin reading at 4:11. From 4:11 through 4:16 there are altogether six verses. In these six verses, we see first that after the Lord ascended into the heavens, He gave to the church some specially gifted persons, such as apostles, prophets, evangelists, and shepherds and teachers. But these specially gifted persons do not build up the church directly; instead, they perfect the saints to build up the church. What does it mean to perfect the saints? It means to feed the saints one by one until they grow up. You might ask me how I know that perfecting the saints here refers to feeding. It is because according to the context, to be perfected is to grow. All mothers know that the most important thing in perfecting a small child is not education but nourishment. When a child is a newborn, the first thing we do is to feed him with milk and give him water to drink. As he gradually grows, we still need to keep giving him nourishment, and that is what we do until he grows up.

Therefore, the first thing in perfecting the saints is to feed them that they may grow, and the second thing is to teach them. We all know that mothers have to teach small children even how to eat. Therefore, I am not saying that doctrines and teachings are useless. What I am saying is that it is wrong to keep teaching your children, yet you do not know how to feed them. It is after they are nourished that you teach them.

Furthermore, as the child gradually grows, you must equip him according to the level of his growth. If you want to teach him to write, then you have to prepare for him a good pencil, a good writing brush, or a good fountain pen; this is to equip him. Thus, perfecting the saints includes three matters: feeding, teaching, and equipping them to be useful.

When I visited the different localities in America, I stayed mostly in the homes of the saints. In the American homes there is one thing that very much impresses me, and even though it is a small thing, it is very practical when applied to the church life. It is that they know how to perfect their children. For example, in one family, one child was only two or three years old, but the father perfected him to do one thing: every morning after the child rose and washed up, the first thing he did was to open the front door, bring in the newspaper, and put it into the newspaper box. This two- or three-year-old boy had been perfected to do this one thing. For six months nothing changed; he did only this one chore. This family had another boy who was assigned to watch over the family's pet dog. Every day the boy watched what the dog ate and how much it ate. The parents fed the boy, and he fed the dog. They also had another boy who was a little older. Every Monday morning he vacuumed the carpet in one room, then on the next day he vacuumed the carpet in another room, and on the following day he vacuumed the carpet in the third room. The oldest child had to cut the grass in the front and back yards. When I stayed with that family and saw the situation, I was very touched. Those saints really knew how to perfect their children. They not only fed them and taught them, but they also equipped them. The result is that the children of that household, whether big or small, all exercised their own function. I feel that a local church should be like this family, with the gifted members perfecting the saints one by one until they all exercise their own function.

ARRIVING AT A FULL-GROWN MAN, AT THE MEASURE OF THE STATURE OF THE FULLNESS OF CHRIST

This does not mean, however, that we will arrive at the goal instantly, because verse 13 says, "Until we all arrive at the oneness of the faith and of the full knowledge of the Son of God, at a full-grown man." We thank the Lord that the young people are progressing, but according to my feeling, you are still very immature and have not yet become grown-up. You have stepped on the right track for growth, but you have not yet grown very much. You still need to grow until all arrive at a full-grown man.

However, we know that the higher a life is, the longer it takes to grow; and the lower the life is, the less time it takes to grow. The lowest life grows the fastest; the higher the life is, the slower it grows. A dog does not need seven years to mature; at most it takes three years. A human child, however, needs twenty-one years to grow to maturity. How long will it take for the new man to become full-grown? I cannot tell, but I want you to know that the life of the new man is higher than the life of our old man. The higher the life, the longer it takes to mature. You young people have risen up to pursue the growth in life today, and that makes me very happy, but you should not have a certain expectation, saying, "Brother Lee has come to give us a training, so we are going to grow up instantly." There is no such thing. Growth requires time because life has a law. However, you should not be disappointed. In any case, you must keep growing.

At the time the church arrives at a full-grown man, it arrives at the measure of the stature of the fullness of Christ.

A full-grown person certainly has the proper measure of the stature of his fullness; these two things are equivalent. There are some particular points here. In this passage the measure of the stature of the fullness of Christ is not mentioned first; rather, it speaks first of the full-grown man. Why is this? For anyone who wants to pursue the growth in life, the first requirement is to take Christ as your person and the second is to take Christ as your life. A full-grown man needs Christ as his person, and a stature with its proper measure needs Christ as life. Taking Christ as our person is the first thing, and taking Christ as life is the second. We all need to learn to go to the Lord and say, "Lord, today I have received mercy and grace to learn to take You as my person. Furthermore, I want to learn to receive grace and mercy with all the brothers and sisters as the one new man, taking You as the person in all of us." This is the highest requirement.

TAKING CARE OF THE UNIVERSAL NEW MAN
IN OUR DAILY WALK

I must take the opportunity at this time to speak a word on taking care of the universal new man in our daily walk. If we have all seen the vision of the new man and have seen that all the churches are not merely individual local churches but the one new man, we will be willing to say, "Lord, I want to receive grace and mercy with all the saints as the one new man, taking You as the person in all of us." If you take Christ in this way as the person of this corporate new man, you will not decide anything in your life by yourself. Because you see that you are a part of the churches as the new man, you will not be able to decide anything merely by yourself. Since you are a part of the new man, your decisions and your living should not be yours; they should be the decisions and the living of the corporate new man. Dear brothers and sisters, this is the ultimate requirement. This is why I say that Christianity has failed the Lord. If the Lord goes to Christianity to look for this new man, He will never find him.

However, we ourselves must also be careful. We say that we are in the Lord's recovery, but if the Lord were to come among us, would He find this new man? This is not merely a matter of individual localities and individual churches; it involves all the churches on earth corporately. Are all the local churches on the earth in the Lord's recovery today truly the one new man? Because the church is a lampstand, you may say that each locality is a lampstand. However, concerning the church being the new man, can you say that each locality is a new man? No, you cannot! All the churches on the earth are the one new man.

In the past we lacked this light, and we did not release this kind of message. Therefore, I do not believe that among us there is one brother or sister who has taken into consideration all the churches on the earth in his or her decision-making and living. Let me ask the brothers from Hong Kong: When you are deciding about a certain matter and living a certain kind of life, as you fellowship, pray, and consider together, do you think about the churches on the whole earth? Have you ever thought of the churches in Australia or in New Zealand? Have you thought of the churches in Germany, England, and other places in Europe? Have you thought of the church in Ghana, Africa? Moreover, have you thought of the churches in Brazil, South America, and the churches in Canada and the United States, North America? Have you ever thought about them in this way? I would dare to guarantee that you have never thought anything like this. At most you have thought about the brothers and sisters in Hong Kong, and you have considered how the brothers and sisters in Hong Kong would feel about your decisions. Although this too is a requirement, it is not a very high one. However, when you put yourselves into the new man and realize that the new man is not only the church in Hong Kong but includes all the churches on the whole earth, you will see that the requirement is extremely high as you consider your decisions and your living.

Thus, I truly hope that from now on every local church, when it is considering, praying, and fellowshipping about a certain decision, will take care of all the churches on the earth and will realize the fact that we are all one new man. Then your decision and living will certainly be of a high standard, requiring you to pay the highest price. Brothers and sisters, may we have eyes to see that this is a requirement we have never had before.

PUTTING ON THE LIFE OF THE UNIVERSAL NEW MAN

I feel that it is the Lord's good pleasure that we have this gathering. Although there are not many from Ghana, Africa nor are there many from Australia and New Zealand, there are at least a few representatives from these places. Thus, every continent is represented here, giving us the position to say that the new man is here. The saved ones in all six continents have representatives here.

Everything is according to the Lord's good pleasure. Two thousand years ago at the time of the apostle Paul, it was quite difficult to speak of the new man being universal. At that time communication and transportation were not well developed. It would have taken several months to go by sailboat from Jerusalem to Rome. Also it would have taken a long time for news from Jerusalem to reach Rome and another length of time for the news from Rome to get back to Jerusalem. Even in the 1800s, when the American missionaries came to China to preach the gospel, they had to spend six months at sea on a ship before they arrived. Today, however, it takes only a short time for Taipei to know what has happened in New York. Anything that happens anywhere in the world is immediately known everywhere else. I feel that this is something well-pleasing to the Lord. We should know how the brothers and sisters in Ghana live, and they also should know how we brothers and sisters here live a spiritual life in righteousness and holiness. We are one new man; we have put on the new man. This new man is not individual, nor is it local; rather, it is universal. When we put on the new man, we put on the universal new man, which was created according to God in righteousness and holiness of the reality. We must ask all the brothers and sisters in all the places: As you are living the church life in your locality and putting on the new man in the Lord's recovery, do you have holiness and righteousness? We all must have the righteousness and holiness of the reality. That righteousness and that holiness are the life of the new man.

GROWING BY TAKING CHRIST AS OUR PERSON

Dear brothers and sisters, do you want to grow? In the past because of our lack of knowledge, our requirements for growth were very low and limited. We said that in order to grow we first would need to go into the Lord's presence to confess our sins. I am not saying that this is wrong. We should first ask the Lord to enlighten us and then confess our sins one by one and apply the Lord's precious blood. After confessing our sins, we need a consecration. Then after consecration, we need to daily ask for the Lord's leading in all matters, great and small. These practices are also right. However, these requirements are not high enough. What should the requirement be? The requirement that is high enough is that we would be for the universal new man. We need to take the Lord Jesus as our person; this includes everything, such as dealing with our sins, consecration, and seeking the will of God.

We truly need message after message to unveil every one of us so that we can see that today in the Lord's recovery we need to become the universal new man, and that we all need to rise up together to take Christ as our person. The brothers and sisters from Japan, the South Sea Islands, Taiwan, Hong Kong, Singapore, Indonesia, Australia, and New Zealand should all take Christ as their person. Whether we are from Europe, North America, South America, or Africa, we all should take Christ as our unique person. When this happens, the new man will be manifested on the earth in righteousness and holiness of the reality. This is the church and the new man. Those of us who are gifted, whether apostles or prophets or evangelists or shepherds and teachers, should all take this as our goal. We must perfect the saints in locality after locality that they may all enter into a situation where they take Christ as their person.

Brothers and sisters, I am truly burdened for this. My hope for you tonight is that you will see in the Bible something that is very high, something which not only Christianity but even we have not as yet touched. We can say that in this training we have only begun to touch this high matter. What is this high matter? It is that the church is not merely the assembling of a group of Christians; the church is the fullness of Christ and the one new man on earth. There is a great old man on this earth, and this old man is the Adamic race, the descendants of Adam. Today on this earth, however, God wants to have another man, the new man.

As I have said, today due to all the technological advances in transportation and communication, which are making progress monthly and even daily, all the peoples of the Adamic race on the entire earth have almost become one. When Hollywood produces something, it becomes popular all over the earth. When America comes out with something new, Hong Kong and Japan get it immediately. This is the universal old man. The Adamic race today has become the universal old man. All the components of this old man are the same in their corruption, evil, filthiness, fornication, and disorderliness. Just as New York is a mess, so are also Paris, Hong Kong, Tokyo, and Copenhagen. Every place is in an equally bad condition. When a new dance comes in, it becomes popular everywhere for a period of time. Consider clothing as an example. Because I am one who travels frequently to many places in the world, I often marvel at what I see. Something that has only recently come into the market in the United States is immediately available in other places. What is this? I tell you, this is taking the devil as the person to bring in the old man, who is dark, evil, and corrupt.

We thank the Lord, though, that today He wants to gain the one new man on earth. Today's Christianity absolutely cannot meet this need. Christianity is full of divisions, and everyone is independent. The Lord's desire is to have the one new man on the earth, so we all need to rise up to take Christ as our corporate person. If we want to make a decision or live a certain kind of life, we cannot decide merely in ourselves; instead, we must take Christ as our person in the new man and with the new man. This requirement is great and high. In this way the new man grows and matures, and we will arrive at a full-grown man.

I repeat, I am very happy to see that most of you brothers and sisters from the Far East are a new generation, and I can tell by listening to you that you have eaten to the full. This is a good sign. In other words, you have gotten onto the proper track for growing. However, you must not forget that this is only the beginning; you must arrive at a full-grown man.

If there is a full-grown man, then there will definitely be the measure of the stature of the fullness of Christ. If you take Christ as your person, then you will surely take Him as your life. Taking Christ as your person is for the new man, while taking Christ as your life is for the Body. If you take Christ as your person, then you will be able to grow and mature. The result will be that the Body of Christ will grow and have the adequate measure of stature as the fullness of Christ. Thus, you can see that as long as we grow and mature, there will be the necessary measure of the stature of the fullness. In other words, if you take Christ as your person, then you will certainly have Christ as your life. Christ as our person is for the growth of the new man; Christ as our life is for the increase of the measure of the stature of the Body.

NOT BEING LITTLE CHILDREN CARRIED ABOUT BY WINDS OF TEACHING

After this, verse 14 continues to say that we should no longer be little children. Let me ask you young brothers and sisters, have you grown up? If you have not grown up, then you are little children. Verse 13 says, "Until we all arrive...at a full-grown man." Then verse 14 says, "That we may be no longer little children tossed by waves and carried about by every wind of teaching." If you are little children, you will be easily carried about by every wind of teaching, but if you have become a grown-up person, you will not be tossed by waves and carried about by the winds of teaching.

What does it say here about where the winds of doctrine come from? How do they blow? The winds of doctrine blow out of the sleight of men in craftiness. In this verse Paul used words with very deep connotations because he had much light and was able to see through the devil's subtleties. We need to see that much of Christianity is in craftiness. If you have the Lord's view and light, you will absolutely say amen to this word. You will see through today's Christianity and realize that it has the sleight, the deceit, of men and that it is involved with craftiness.

What does this mean? God's eternal purpose is that His redeemed ones may become His one Body for Him to obtain His fullness and that they may also become the one new man for God's economy to be lived out on earth. This is God's intention, and this is the Lord's eternal purpose. However, everything Christianity does today completely destroys this purpose. You must know that many zealous Christians today who are working for the Lord do not mean to be crafty or deceitful. In their love for the Lord their desire is to be zealous, but they have been tricked by the subtle one. Behind them is a deceiver with his sleight. It is very evident that today's Christian workers have caused Christians to become divided. How do they do this? It is by preaching good doctrines to them. A certain good-sounding doctrine can divide a group of Christians. Many have absolutely no concept concerning the Body of Christ and the new man. On the surface they are preaching biblical doctrines to people, which is a good thing. Nevertheless, underneath and behind this good thing is the sleight of Satan.

From this point of view, you can see that there are many groups in Christianity, each of which seems to be doing good things because they are preaching the gospel, teaching the truth, saving people, helping people, and teaching people to know the Bible. Who would have thought that underneath and behind these good things there is Satan's craftiness and sleight? By this sleight many Christians are fully divided. Many members of these groups do not have an ear to hear when you try to talk to them about the truth of the Body or the new man. Not only do they refuse to listen, but they also turn around to oppose and condemn you. Is this not craftiness? Is this not deception? Many doctrines, many teachings, many groups, and many practices in today's Christianity appear to be for Christ, but in reality they are simply the sleight of men and craftiness that divide the Lord's people.

Here I must use as an example an event that took place among us fifteen or sixteen years ago. At that time a few among us were influenced by a certain spiritual man, and these few shouted the slogan that they had seen the full Christ; they claimed that they were those with a vision. Some of the brothers and sisters at that time were shaken by what was said. Today almost twenty years have passed. History has become facts, and the facts prevail over everything. Look around; where have those people gone who shouted that they had the vision? They have divided again and again on this island. I cannot tell you how many times they have divided. During the ten years from 1957 to 1967 they damaged at least one or two hundred useful young people. During this time their craftiness was not to damage the useless ones; they sought to damage only the promising ones. On the surface, they said they had seen the vision of the full Christ, but secretly they were doing this kind of damaging work.

At this time I must expose Satan's craftiness and show you that this is today's Christianity. Therefore, I would advise you not to readily follow those who shout various slogans nor quickly listen to what others say. No liar will ever tell you that he is lying. Every liar will tell others that he is speaking the truth. All of Christianity today is in a deception, in that so-called Christian workers put people under their control and thus divide the Body of Christ. As long as they can arrive at this goal, they do not care about their methods. This is why you must be clear about one matter: Do not listen when others tell you this or that. Ignore any slogans, and remember only one thing—one Body and one new man. If anyone wants to make them two, we cannot agree. How many new men are there? One new man. How many Bodies are there? One Body. There is one Body and one new man. If anyone tries to produce two, that must be false; if anyone tries to divide, that must be a deception. One Body and one new man. It is one in all of Indonesia, one in all of Thailand, one in all of Southeast Asia, and one on the entire earth. If someone makes another one, regardless of how real it looks outwardly, it must be false because there is only one Body and one new man.

This is why Ephesians says that we should no longer be little children carried about by the winds of teaching, which are not necessarily the winds of heretical teaching but may be winds of proper teaching. How do those winds of teaching blow? They blow in the sleight of men and in craftiness to bring people into a system of schemes and error. The system here is Satan's system, and the schemes and errors here are systematized. All divisions and damage are plots, made not by men but by the devil, who is behind men. The devil utilizes the craftiness and sleight of men to bring people into his system of schemes and error.

From this we all can arrive at the conclusion that by having been enlightened and seen a vision, we know that today the Lord wants nothing other than one Body and one new man. For the Body, we must take Him as our life; for the one new man, we must take Him as our person. When we all truly take Him as the person of the universal new man, we will be willing to pay any price. We will grow, and we will also experience Him as our life. Then the stature of the Body will grow in its measure. Then at this point, we will have to be on guard against the craftiness of the enemy.

Over the past ten or more years, it seems that we have become seriously ill due to that incident that happened among us. You must know that after your body goes through a serious illness and recovers, its resistance to that particular sickness is strengthened. We thank the Lord. I believe that today the churches in the Lord's recovery all have such a resistance against that kind of thing. If it happens again, we certainly will know how to swallow up that craftiness and not be deceived by it again.

CHAPTER SEVEN

ONE NEW MAN APPEARING IN ALL THE EARTH

Scripture Reading: Eph. 4:13-16; 1 Cor. 12:14-17

THE FOUR-LEVEL MEANING OF THE CHURCH—
ASSEMBLY, HOUSE, BODY, MAN

The Chinese term for *church* readily conveys the meaning of the church as being a congregation. We cannot say that to understand the church as a congregation is wrong, but this concept is too human, natural, and religious. According to the human, natural, and religious concepts, the church is a human congregation related to a belief or a religion; it is a religious congregation. If we speak according to the scriptural utterance, however, the church is the house of God, or preferably the household, the family, of God. The house refers to mainly the dwelling place, and the household, the family, refers to the members of the house. This utterance gives the meaning of the church according to the Bible. First Timothy 3:15 speaks of the house of God, the church of the living God. The church as the house of God is both His dwelling place and His family.

This utterance is a little higher than the common concept, but it is not high enough. A higher view is that the church is the Body of Christ. This is very high, but it also is not high enough. From the time the Brethren in England were raised up in the last century, all these aspects of the church have been made known. They saw that the church is the assembly of the called-out ones, that the church is the house of God, and that the church is the Body of Christ. But the Bible does not stop here in speaking about this matter of the church. There is still a higher utterance in the Bible, and that is that the church is the one new man, a man. You need to see now that the church is an assembly, a house, a Body, and a man.

In an assembly as a congregation we are all members. But what is required of the members of a congregation? They need to love one another: We are all in one congregation; as we are all members of this congregation, we should love one another. I have heard this kind of speaking from the time I was a young boy. In Christianity, most of the speaking is concerning the church being a group of people who are of the same persuasion. The Presbyterian Church, the Baptist Church, the Methodist Church, the Lutheran Church, and the Episcopalian Church all say that each one is a member, so they must love one another.

When we advance a little, we say that the church is the house of God. The house is more intimate than a congregation or an assembly. Loving one another as members of a congregation is a far cry from loving one another as members of a household, a family. If I introduce someone as a member of my family, you know that the relationship here is much more intimate.

We would think that this is already good enough, but it is not high enough. When we advance further, we see that the church is the Body. In the Body it is a matter not of intimately loving one another but of being members one of another. Although there may be distinctions among the members, they absolutely cannot be separated. The hand and the arm are distinct, but they are inseparable. Two brothers are members of the same family and can play together when they are happy. But when they are not happy with each other, they separate; one goes to the beach at Keelung and the other goes to Mount Ali. But the arm and the hand absolutely cannot separate. They cannot even go into two adjacent rooms separately, let alone go to two different places such as the beach and the mountain, because once they are separated, they are finished.

Ultimately the Bible speaks of the church as the one new man. I cannot find any type that stands for the new man. In the Body we have the members; in the household we have the family members; in the assembly we have the assembly members. But what do we have in the man? The only thing is the person. In the new man, there is nothing but the person. This level is so high that it cannot be higher, so strict it cannot be stricter, and so intimate it cannot be more intimate. All are one new man; this one new man has only one person, and this person is the Lord Jesus.

ALL THE CHURCHES ON EARTH
AS ONE NEW MAN BEING POSSIBLE
ACCORDING TO THE LORD'S WORD

Dear brothers and sisters, I am looking to the Lord from the depths of my being that at this time when saints from all the six continents are meeting together here, we would all seize the opportunity to see the highest meaning of the church revealed in the Bible. The highest definition of the church in the Bible is the new man. On the cross the Lord slew the enmity and created both the Jewish and Gentile believers in Himself into one new man. Dear brothers and sisters, is this believable? Is this possible? Can all the believers on the earth, with respect to time from antiquity to the present and with respect to space from east to west and from north to south, possibly become one man? Humanly speaking, this is impossible. Many of us are married. We know that even two people as husband and wife cannot become one person. Even though the Bible says that the husband and wife should become one flesh, many times the husband is the husband and the wife is the wife; the two cannot become one. Now we want people from all six continents, people with different colors of skin—white, black, yellow, and brown— to become one. Humanly speaking, I may be the first not to believe; I simply cannot believe this. We cannot even be one as the assembly, let alone one as the new man. If we cannot be one as the assembly, it is really hard to say that we all can be the one new man!

In the past, some people poured cold water on me and advised me not to believe what I believe. What do I believe? I believe that, first, the church is the assembly; second, the church is the house; third, the church is the Body; and, lastly, the highest aspect, the church is the new man. I believe this because the Bible says this. But some people with good intentions poured cold water on this, saying that this is impossible.

For example, in 1957 I released more than thirty messages here in Taipei concerning the ground of the church, and after releasing them I went to Manila. At that time, there was a brother in Manila who was twenty years older than I; he was an old English missionary working there. One day I gave a message about the church today being the miniature of the New Jerusalem. After I released this message, this man came to me with his good intentions and said, "Brother Lee, you certainly are not speaking of today but of the future." I had clearly stated that the church today is the miniature of the New Jerusalem. I had distinctly asserted that it is today, but he still came to say, "Brother Lee, you mean in the future, not today; it is impossible today." Inwardly I said, "You believe it is impossible, so for you it is impossible. But I believe it is possible." Do you understand what I mean? When he spoke this word, I did not answer him; I just let it go.

Again in the same year, 1957, after the release of the messages on the ground of the church, we all saw the matter of "one locality, one church." Therefore, the elders of the church in Taipei suggested that we do our best to be open and fellowship with the three or four other groups, which may be called "free groups," that were meeting in Taipei in the Lord's name. Since they were not in religion and were non-denominational, why would they not come and meet together with us in the city of Taipei to become the one testimony? All the elders agreed and sent two or three representatives to visit these few Christian groups to invite their representatives to come for fellowship. One day all the representatives from these groups came to the elders' room in meeting hall number one in Taipei, and I was also present. The elders said to the representatives of these groups, "We would really like to ask that we all be one." Our elders even made such an offer: "You may think that we have too many people and too much power so that once you and we become one, you will be swallowed up. Therefore, before the Lord, we are willing to give up our responsibilities as elders and turn them over to you, as long as you are willing to get rid of all your differing matters.

First, you will be the elders instead of us. Second, we will give you the deed to the property." We can say that we laid everything out on the table. The number of attendants in these three or four groups added together did not equal one fourth of our number, nor could their property be compared to ours because we had a great deal of property. Yet the elders were willing and happy to give up their positions and responsibilities as elders and let the elders of the one united church preside over the church affairs. At this point, they had nothing to say. What was there left to say? They were all silent for a moment, then someone said, "Brothers, this is good, but we would still like to meet in our own meetings." Once this leader said this, everyone followed him to say the same thing.

I absolutely believe that from that time on, their criticizing mouths were sealed. We would have given them everything, and all that we asked for in return was the oneness. In the end, however, they still said that although it was good, they would rather meet in their own meetings. During this time, a brother from among them opened his mouth and said, "When you speak of fallen Christianity, you always denounce others for being fallen." I immediately answered, "Brother, if today's Christianity is not fallen, then what is fallen? Fallen Christianity refers not only to others but also to us. If we are fallen, then we too are fallen Christianity. Today it is not a matter of denouncing or not denouncing. The question today is whether or not we are standing on a fallen ground." I am telling you this to testify to you that the concept in today's fallen Christianity is that the church today is not able to come up to the standard. They think it is impossible.

I can also tell you that when I go to Europe or America, I frequently meet Christians with whom I sit down and fellowship. When we speak of the truth and reach a conclusion, they cannot deny that this is the truth. But they say, "Even though this is the truth, there is no way to practice it today, so we can only wait for that day." Sometimes I have asked them, "When will that day be?" They are unable to say when that day will be. I have said, "After the church age is over, it will be the kingdom age, and we will not be able to practice the church in the kingdom age. After the kingdom age is over, it will be the New Jerusalem, and in the New Jerusalem we will not need to practice the church. So when exactly will the day be when we will have the practice of the church?" They were unable to answer me and could only say, "It is true that the Bible says so, but it is impossible today."

I would like to ask you, brothers and sisters, do you believe that it is possible today, or do you believe that it is impossible? I have already said that I am the first to say that according to the natural concept it is impossible; according to the Lord's Word, however, I am the first to believe that it is possible. Previously in America I could not say that the situation was possible, but I can testify that today for the most part it is possible, and this possibility is being manifested. Yet there are some opposers who criticize, saying, "Why do you listen only to that one man? You receive anything Brother Lee says, and you feel that anything not spoken by Brother Lee has a problem. How can all of you be so foolish as to follow that little Chinaman?" You can see how pitiful today's Christianity truly is. When I first went to America, I told those criticizing brothers about this testimony, and they said it was impossible. After more than ten years, the possibility is being manifested, but they are still unwilling to give in. Furthermore, they begin to criticize and condemn us by saying that the people in the Lord's recovery are foolish to follow a man. Sometimes when I hear what the opposers say, it makes me want to laugh. I tell them, "Why don't you be this way? It won't hurt you to try!" Some said, "I cannot do it." Then I said, "We thank and praise the Lord that there are some who can." Brothers and sisters, do you think this is something done by man? No, this is not man's doing.

At this time I have a burden and hope that you all will see the vision that all the churches on the entire earth will be the one new man; this is definitely possible. Our Lord never speaks anything in vain; He will certainly do everything according to what He has spoken, and whatever He has spoken will come to pass. He has said that there will be one new man, so there will be one new man. It was not accomplished in the last century, nor has it been accomplished in this century, but there will be a century in which it will come to pass. It was not done yesterday, and maybe will not be done today, but it will definitely happen tomorrow. Do not forget that He is the Lord. His word will never return void. Men, Satan, and all the demons can only prolong the time, but they cannot make His word void. The Lord said that the church is the new man, so the church eventually has to be the new man.

In America there are several thousand brothers and sisters. If the devil comes and says, "You Christians are not one!", I certainly have the assurance that these few thousand brothers and sisters in America would all stand up to say, "We are one! We are not merely one assembly, one household, and one Body; we are also one man!" Brothers and sisters, can you now all say together, "We are one new man"? You can! Yes, we are one new man.

HENCEFORTH THE LORD DEFINITELY MAKING ALL THE CHURCHES ON THE EARTH INTO ONE NEW MAN

I absolutely believe that this conference and training are symbolic. In the past we had international conferences, but in none were all the continents represented. At this time, however, all the continents are represented; this is of the Lord. This is a symbol that henceforth the Lord wants to raise up the churches of His recovery in all the cities, towns, and localities on the earth and make them all into one new man. Please consider: Can you believe this or not? It does not matter whether or not you can believe; the Lord's word is faithful. This is not my invention nor my creation nor my imagination; this is what the Lord has said in His Word. He has slain the enmity on the cross, creating the two in Himself into one new man. I believe that before the Lord returns this will be fulfilled.

Now, dear brothers and sisters, you and I have all seen that this is not just a matter of being united, nor is it merely to say that we all stand on the ground of one locality with one church, and therefore we are one. This morning we all must see that we are one new man and that the churches in all the localities on earth are one new man. We are not simply one assembly, nor are we merely one household, nor are we even merely one Body; we are one new man. In the assembly there is a distinction among the members, in the family there is a distinction among the members, and in the Body there is also a distinction among the members. In the new man, however, there is no distinction. In the Body we are members one of another, in the family we are brothers and sisters as family members one of another, and in the assembly we are also members one of another. In the new man, however, there is nothing of mutuality. In the new man there is only one matter, the person.

Dear brothers and sisters, I would like to ask you again, do you believe this is possible? I believe it! I believe it because this is not my dream or imagination; this is what I have found out in reading God's Word. He has created the two in Himself into one new man. Brothers and sisters from Africa, America, Germany, and Australia, do you believe this? You do believe it! Brothers and sisters from Japan, do you believe it? You also believe it! Brothers and sisters from Manila, do you believe that all the saints on the entire earth can be one new man? You believe it! O Lord! One new man! I believe that the one new man is possible. This is possible; the Bible tells me so, and we must believe what it says. Since the Bible says this is so, it will definitely be fulfilled. God has said it is so, so it will be fulfilled accordingly.

In God's view, one thousand years is not much different from two thousand years. To God, time is not a problem. If we do not accomplish this for Him between 1970 and 1980, He will wait for the period from 1980 to 1990. If we still do not give Him the opportunity, He will wait for the time between 1990 and 2000. No matter what, this new man must appear. I am not afraid that you do not believe, but I do hope that you all would believe because this will be a blessing to you. If you do not believe, then one day God will carry it out with another group of people after you. I believe that one day there will be a new man on the earth. That will be a glorious day.

I believe that all the advances of civilization and technology, such as the train, the automobile, the airplane, the telegraph, and even the telephone are all for this new man. The things that happen in the churches in Ghana, Africa can be known immediately by the churches in every other locality. The new technological inventions have already shrunk the earth in the matter of distance. I believe that in the future the distances will be reduced even more. Today if I want to make a long-distance phone call to America, all I need is modern telecommunication equipment to be able to dial directly from Taipei. Twenty years ago if we wanted to make a long-distance phone call, we had to make a trip to the Telegraph Bureau. Now all I need to do is dial from my home, and the operator will connect me. One day, however, we will not even need the operator; I will be able to dial your number directly from my home. I believe that these things are not merely for the world; all these things are for the church. There is definitely the possibility that the saints in all the localities in all their environmental circumstances will become the one new man.

THE SECRET TO BECOMING THE ONE NEW MAN

Now we must come to see how we can become the one new man. It is not by any method, ordinance, or organization. It is not by any of these. Ephesians 4:13-16 is a very short passage of the Bible, but the entire secret is contained here. The secret that all the saints on the entire earth will become the one new man depends first on holding to truth in love. Do not take this word lightly. Is the practice of head covering the truth, the reality? Everyone must see that head covering in itself is not the truth. Behind head covering there is a truth, and that is that Christ is our Head with His headship. Sisters, do not hold to the head covering you are wearing. I do not oppose your wearing it; when you are praying, you should wear a head covering, but this is not the truth, the reality. The reality is that Christ is the Head with the headship, and this is the truth we hold to.

Likewise, with regard to the matter of baptism, neither sprinkling nor immersion is the reality; the truth is that we have been buried and raised together with Christ. We must hold to this truth in love. All the outward ordinances and methods are not the reality. You should never argue over the method, but you should hold to truth in love. Simply stated, the truth is Christ. Holding to truth is holding to Christ.

Next, we must grow up into Christ in all things. Brothers and sisters, regardless of whether you are from Africa or Australia and regardless of whether you are white, yellow, or black, we all must grow up into Christ in all things. Here *all things* means every single thing, whether big or small; we must grow up into Christ in all things. Even today there are still many things in which we are not in Christ but are outside of Christ. We need to grow up into Christ in all things, both big and small. You have Christ in you, but there are still many things in you that have not grown up into Christ. This is entirely a matter of the Spirit. To grow up into Christ is to grow up into the Spirit. Your speaking must be in the Spirit; your actions, your adornment, and your attire must all be in the Spirit; your dealings with others, your managing of affairs, and the way you treat people must be in the Spirit. You need to get into the Spirit in all things.

We need to hold to Christ as the truth and grow into Christ, the life-giving Spirit, in all things. This will make us the new man. If we grow up into Christ in all things, then in Christ there will not be this kind of person or that kind of person. There will not be any kind of person but Christ, who is all and in all. This is the new man. When we hold to Christ as the truth in love and grow up into Him in all things, then we will no longer be many different kinds of people. When we grow up into Christ in all things, we all will be just one in Christ. This is the one new man.

Verse 16 continues by saying that the whole Body is from Him and out of Him, something that comes out from Him. If you have never grown up into Him, then you could never come out from Him. Verse 15 says that we must grow up into Him in all things, and verse 16 says that all the Body comes from Him and out of Him. Brothers and sisters, we must see that in all the localities we are doing only one thing, and that is to minister Christ and to pray that others may hold to Christ as the truth in love and grow up into Him in all things. Eventually, there will not be this kind of people or that kind of people, but there will be only Christ. This is the new man. When we grow up into Christ in this way, spontaneously we will allow Christ to be the person. Christ as the person is not individual or local, but universal.

The churches in our different localities do not have strict rules to regulate us to be the same and to make us all do the same thing. However, because the brothers and sisters in every place all hold to Christ as truth in love and grow up into Him in all things, the result is that we all spontaneously take Christ as the person. If you grow up into Christ in all things, then He is your person. If all the brothers and sisters in all six continents take Christ as the person, then spontaneously all the brothers and sisters on the earth in His recovery will be the one new man.

WITH ONE HEART AND ONE MOUTH
SPEAKING THE SAME THING

When that happens, even though we all are many, when we speak, it will be with one mouth because we will all speak the same thing. You will not have to teach me something first, and also I will not have to tell you anything; yet we will speak the same thing.

A sister from Anaheim testified that when she first came to Los Angeles in 1969 and was invited to the brothers' houses and sisters' houses, they were speaking the same thing in all the different houses. She thought this was very strange. She wondered that maybe those who were in the one house had phoned beforehand those who were in the other house in order to know what to speak. Later she realized that that was not possible. The day will come when even the angels and the demons will be surprised that you in Africa are speaking exactly the same thing as those in Australia. Although we are many, our mouth is one.

Once when I spoke about having one heart and one mouth, I asked, "Whose is this mouth?" Someone said very softly, "It is your own." You are wrong; your understanding is wrong. Having one heart and one mouth means that even though we are many and all are speaking, we all speak the same thing. Some say it in Spanish, some in Portuguese, some in Italian, some in English, some in French, some in the southern Fukien dialect, and some in the Shantung dialect. We all are speaking in many languages and with many accents, but we are speaking one thing. This is what it means to have one mouth.

If the Lord allows, I truly hope you all will go out to travel to Ghana, Brazil, Germany, and Italy to take a look; after seeing these localities, you will inwardly worship the Lord because you will see that in the entire earth there is one new man with one heart and one mouth speaking the same thing. Who taught them this? It is not a matter of their being taught, but a matter of their growth. This thing cannot be taught; rather, it comes from growth. I believe this is absolutely possible.

I do not know where the next international conference will be, but I do know that in that day the manifestation of the new man will be higher and more intensified. I definitely believe that the Lord's word will not return to Him void and that His word will accomplish God's heart's desire on the earth. Since God has released this word in this training, He will definitely not allow this word to return to Him void. When you go back to your localities, you will certainly live in this word. How will you live? By holding to truth, to reality, in love and by growing up into Christ the Head in all things, that is, by taking Him as your person. The result, regardless of whether it is in Australia, Africa, America, Asia, or Europe, will be that without any planning in advance we will all speak the same thing and have the same expression. How glorious! This is the one new man!

CHAPTER EIGHT

EXPERIENCING CHRIST TO BE JOINED AND KNIT TOGETHER

Scripture Reading: Eph. 4:13-16, 22-24

THE FIRST APPEARING OF THE CHURCH BEING IN AN INTERNATIONAL GROUP OF PEOPLE

The first time the church was established on the earth was on the day of Pentecost. The works of God are all under His sovereign authority, and His sovereign authority is in all His works. On the day of Pentecost, when the church in Jerusalem was established, it was established not merely with the inhabitants of Jerusalem, but with peoples from all over the world who were gathered together at Jerusalem. There were speakers of at least fourteen or fifteen dialects gathered together that day. Thus, the first appearing of the church was among a group of people from many different places and countries who spoke many different languages. In a matter of moments, all those people from so many places and countries, who spoke so many different languages, became one new man. They were all speaking the same kind of language there. Anything man does requires gradual improvement, and what comes last is the best; however, what God does, does not need improvement; it is the best from the first moment. The first appearing of the church was at its highest standard. This is very significant. The first appearing of the church was not merely among a local group of people; instead, it was among an international group of people. We thank God that we here in this conference are not merely a group of people from one locality. The regions represented here today are even more widespread than those represented by the people in Jerusalem at that time. Hallelujah! If we were to invite representatives present here from each of the six continents to the platform, we could ask them to use their native languages to speak the same thing. This demonstration would give us a deep impression of the new man among an international group of people.

THE LORD DESIRING TO RECOVER THE TESTIMONY OF THE NEW MAN ON THE EARTH TODAY

I absolutely believe that this international gathering is not a coincidence but the Lord's arrangement. At this time we have received a deep impression that the Lord in these days is moving in His recovery. I myself feel it is marvelous to be able to release these messages on the new man, which have never before been released. Even during the conference preceding this training, I was not clear as to what I should speak in this five-day training. It was not until the first day that I became clear within that the Lord wants us to take the opportunity to release the messages on the new man, while representatives from all six continents are present. I believe that from now on the churches in all the six continents will no longer be the same as before, and the churches will go on in the way of the new man. We all must arrive at this goal of being the one new man in the whole earth, speaking the same thing with one heart and one mouth to the glory of God.

Christianity has been bearing a negative testimony for several centuries by constantly saying that Christians have no way to be one. But today the Lord wants to present a positive testimony for Christianity to see that Christians can certainly be one. Brothers and sisters, can Christians really be one? By the Lord's grace it is more than possible! In a previous message I used negative words to speak of positive matters. I said that it is impossible even for a husband and wife to arrive at the true oneness, much less possible for individual believers. Without the Lord's mercy and grace, all of us descendants of Adam are "little demons," and no one can be one with anyone else. But on the day of Pentecost the Lord came in, and those speakers of different dialects immediately became one in the Lord. We thank the Lord that all of us have been baptized into the Triune God. Every one of us can boast, "Hallelujah, today I am in Christ. In Christ we all have the Lord and His grace, so we are all one. We can be one; this is absolutely possible!" It is possible because we are all in the Lord and have His grace.

If we look at ourselves, there is no way for us to be one with others. Therefore, we should not look at ourselves, and the Lord never asks us to look at ourselves. The Lord wants us to look at Him. The Lord says, "Look to Me and you will be saved." As soon as we look at the Lord, we are immediately one in the Lord. Therefore, we can all testify together today that it is possible for Christians to be one. Moreover, it is not only possible; we are already practicing it. The two days of gospel meetings that we had during the conference would not have been possible in a mere Christianity alliance. In the Lord's church there is no need for an alliance because we are already one. This is a symbol, a sign. I really believe it when I say that from now on the Lord will go the same way and do the same work in each of the six continents; He will sound the same trumpet and produce the same testimony.

THE APPEARING OF THE NEW MAN
BEING ENTIRELY A MATTER OF SPIRITUAL LIFE

In this message I want to give a further word of fellowship. Please remember that the appearing of this new man is not a movement. Rather, it is entirely a matter of spiritual life, and this spiritual life is our Lord Jesus truly and practically being our life. It is not that you stir me up and I stir you up; instead, it is that each of us lives out Christ by enjoying and experiencing Him. This is altogether a story of Christ's life. On the one hand, we are now excited because we have seen that the six continents have become one new man. On the other hand, however, we do not want to have any outward activity because of our excitement. What we want is to experience Christ inwardly as our life and thus spontaneously produce the new man as its result. We are the new man. The reason we are the new man is that each of us has Christ in us as our life.

Some in Christianity say that the new man cannot be

realized. This is because they do not know Christ as their life; at the most they know Christ as their Savior. But today in the Lord's recovery the Lord wants to have an absolute, thorough, and complete recovery of the all-inclusive Spirit as our daily life. Regardless of which continent we come from, we each must live by this all-inclusive Christ daily in reality, and this is done by taking Him as our life and our person. Moment by moment we enjoy Him, experience Him, and allow Him to live out of us; therefore, in Him we cannot be anything else but one. We do not need to endeavor to be united; we are one spontaneously. "For as many of you as were baptized into Christ have put on Christ. There cannot be Jew nor Greek, there cannot be slave nor free man, there cannot be male and female; for you are all one in Christ Jesus" (Gal. 3:27-28). We are one new man. This is not a movement, a stirring up, or an organization. We are one new man because we live by Christ and allow Him to live out of us. Even though we are of different nationalities, races, and languages, we have one thing in common: Christ is our life.

Ephesians 4:14-15 says, "That we may be no longer little children tossed by waves and carried about by every wind of teaching in the sleight of men, in craftiness with a view to a system of error, but holding to truth in love, we may grow up into Him in all things, who is the Head, Christ." Then verse 16 continues to say, "Out from whom all the Body, being joined together and being knit together." First we grow up into Him; then we are out from Him. First there is the growing into Him, and then there is the coming out from Him. In any organization there are liaison officers, but in the church we do not need such liaison officers because Christ is our "liaison." We can be joined and knit together because the entire Body is out from Him. If we want to be out from Him, however, we must first grow up into Him. When you grow up into Christ in all things, then out from Him you can spontaneously be joined and knit together with all the saints. If we are not in Christ, or if we have not grown up into Christ in so many things, then we cannot be joined together even with our own flesh brothers. If, however, we have grown up into Christ in all things, then we can be joined together. One brother may be from Ghana, Africa, and another brother may be from Taipei, Taiwan. They come from two different places that are distant from each other, and they have different customs, skin colors, languages, and concepts, yet when they meet each other, there is something within them that joins them together. They do not need a liaison in order to be joined together because they have already been joined together. They both have grown up into Christ in all things, and now they are joined and knit together out from Him.

THE LORD'S ECONOMY BEING NOT EVOLUTION BUT TRANSFORMATION

Moreover, I would like to say that in the Lord's economy there is no evolution; evolution is of the devil. In the Lord's economy, however, there is transformation. The Lord Jesus, who is the all-inclusive Spirit, can transform people. Christianity cannot transform anyone. Religion can only teach people, adorn them, and do a cosmetic work on them. As far as human society is concerned, religion is good. However, the Lord's economy is not a matter of religion but a matter of the living Spirit. The all-inclusive Christ as the life-giving Spirit has come into us. He does not come to "beautify our faces"; rather, He comes to transform us.

According to the Bible, God's economy is transformation. How are we transformed? It is not through teachings but by our Lord who accomplished everything by His death and resurrection. He accomplished whatever He needed, and He accomplished whatever we needed; He accomplished everything that both God and man needed. Then He became the all-inclusive life-giving Spirit. The Spirit gets into anyone who calls on the Lord's name, and then He operates and works in him in many ways to transform him. The Lord truly can transform people; this is something I have experienced myself. We are of different nationalities with different customs and different backgrounds. The reason we can become one new man is that the Lord has done a transformation work in us. The Lord truly transforms us. Even with the highest doctrines none of us can change ourselves.

When I first went to America, the Lord gave me the

wisdom to see that I was not going there to sell my "Chinese goods," but that I was going to supply Christ to people. Therefore, I did not speak doctrines to them. I preached what I had experienced and supplied them with what I myself had eaten. On the one hand, I supplied them with Christ, and on the other hand, I ate the Christ whom I supplied. This Christ transformed me inwardly, and He also transformed them inwardly. Therefore, it was easy for us to be blended together. This is not to say that I have been Americanized, but that I have been "Christized," and they also have been "Christized." This is not a matter of mere wisdom; this is a matter of transformation.

Not only are the Chinese and the Americans different, but even the northern Chinese and the southern Chinese have many differences. In 1933 when I went from northern China to Shanghai, Brother Nee and the co-workers called a special meeting for me. After the messages many people came to fellowship with me. They spoke the Shanghai dialect, and I could not understand them at all. Nevertheless, whether or not I could understand, I talked with them. In the end they understood me, and I understood them because Christ was in them and in me. Although we could not understand the dialect very well, we really knew what we were talking about, so it was easy for us to become the new man and speak the same thing. Today we also are speaking about the new man.

Today we all must see that this is not merely a conference of all the continents in which we decide what we all will speak about from now on. Absolutely not. Instead, it is a matter of all of us seeing that the Lord is our life and our person. The Lord today wants to show Satan that He can produce the one new man out of every tongue and people from among the nations. It is not an outward teaching or an outward movement, but it is He Himself within us as life and as our person. We all receive Him and grow up into Him in all things, and then the whole Body is joined and knit together out from Him.

Dear brothers and sisters, perhaps you would ask me, "Is there anything in the first few verses in Ephesians 4 that speaks about transformation?" No, there is nothing, but if you go on to verse 23, there is something about transformation. We grow up into Him, and then come out from Him; this is transformation. No one can grow into Christ and come out from Christ without being transformed. Only by holding to truth in love and growing up into the Head, Christ, in all things can the entire Body be joined and knit together out from Him. When we are joined and knit together, we are transformed. The Chinese brothers will be the same as the brothers from Ghana; the brothers from all the different countries will have been transformed to be the same. I absolutely believe this. When we are all transformed, all the cultures, backgrounds, customs, and languages will be swallowed up by Christ. This is the glory of Christ. A brother from Ghana, Africa will speak, sing, fellowship, and praise with a brother from Germany; this is the glory of Christ. I believe that this word is a prophecy of what will happen in the next ten years.

In ten years you will see that many people speaking many different languages will be able to fellowship, praise, and proclaim the Lord's holy name together. At this time only a few brothers have come from Africa, but I certainly believe that one day hundreds and even thousands will come together. When we grow up into Christ in all things, the entire Body will be joined and knit together out from Him. When we grow up into Him and come out from Him, then we will be completely in Him and not in ourselves. In ourselves we have no way. Furthermore, not to mention the Chinese and the Americans, even you who are from the same island and from the same home cannot be one. Out from yourselves there is no way to be joined and knit together, but when we grow up into Him and come out from Him, we are easily joined and knit together. You and I and all must grow up into Him, pass through Him, and come out from Him; then there will be this new man.

PUTTING OFF THE OLD MAN
AND PUTTING ON THE NEW MAN

Verses 22 and 24 continue to say that we must put off the old man and put on the new man. The old man refers to our old social life. To put off the old man means to put off this old social life. Putting on the new man refers to putting on the church life. The old social life is just the old man, while the new church life is the new man. Many in Christianity do not know this matter. The Revised Standard Version of the Bible, which was published in the 1940s, translates *the old man* in Ephesians 4 as "your old nature" and *the new man* as "the new nature." In this view, putting off the old man means putting off the old nature, while putting on the new man means putting on the new nature. This shows that many in Christianity do not have the proper knowledge of the church as the new man. The Lord's salvation today causes us to put off not merely our old nature but our old social life. The Lord's salvation today does not cause us merely to put on a new nature, but it causes us to put on the church life. Putting off the old man and putting on the new man mean to put off our old social life and put on the church life. The old social life has many different kinds of backgrounds. There are the Japanese social life, the Chinese social life, the South American social life, the North American social life, the Southeast Asian social life, and so on. The old social life is of different kinds. However, I tell you that the church life is unique; there is only one kind. In the Lord's life and in Him as the all-inclusive Spirit, we are putting off the old social life and putting on the new church life. The result is that in the church life we are the new man. This is not an outward reformation or an outward movement, but it is a transformation of our living from within.

How is the putting off of the old man and the putting on of the new man accomplished? The key is in verse 23, which says, "And that you be renewed in the spirit of your mind." It is hard to say if this spirit is our human spirit or the Spirit of Christ; it must be the two spirits mingled as one spirit. This tells us that in order to put off our old social life and put on the new church life, we need to open our spirit within and allow the Spirit of Christ to fill, saturate, and permeate our entire spirit until the Spirit overflows into our mind, emotion, and will. It is by this overflowing Spirit that we can be renewed, and this renewing is transformation. Transformation is not the result of any outward teaching; rather, it is the issue

of the Spirit's saturating, permeating, watering, and processing. The life-giving Spirit enters our spirit to process us, and
this processing is transformation because the element of the
Spirit increases. It is this mingled spirit—the spirit that is
two spirits becoming one spirit—that seeps out of our spirit
and soaks through our mind, emotion, and will, even our
entire being. In this way we are renewed in this spirit of
our mind. The renewing makes us all into the new man. In
this renewing we put off the old social life and put on the
church life. This is putting off the old man and putting on
the new man.

The Lord today is doing this work on the earth, and this is
the goal of the Lord's recovery today. All those who love Him,
pursue Him, and follow Him on the entire earth today must
be renewed in the spirit of their mind to become the one new
man, taking Him as their person and living by Him. This is
what the Lord wants today.

DRINKING OF THE SPIRIT

Scripture Reading: Eph. 4:3-4; 1 Cor. 12:13; 6:17; Phil. 1:19b; Eph. 4:23; 2 Tim. 4:22a

There is one Body and one Spirit. I absolutely believe that at this time the Lord's Spirit has led us to touch the matter of the Body, and from the Body to touch the new man. What we saw in the past was not very clear. Ephesians speaks of the Body at the very beginning and continues to speak of the Body, connecting it to the new man. Whenever it speaks of the Body, it connects it to the new man. We have seen not only the one Body but also the one new man. Now we can say, "One Body, one new man, and one Spirit." In this message we will fellowship about the Spirit.

THE SPIRIT BEING THE LIFE OF THE BODY
AND THE PERSON OF THE NEW MAN

We know that the Body needs life, and the new man needs a person. With regard to the church as the Body of Christ, there is the need for Christ to be our life; with regard to the church as the new man, there is the need for Christ to be our person. At this time we want to point out clearly that on the one hand, the Spirit is life, and on the other hand, He is a person. The Spirit is not only life to us, but also a person. In the New Testament, you can find certain passages that emphasize the Spirit as life. For example, the Lord said, "It is the Spirit who gives life;...the words which I have spoken to you are spirit and are life" (John 6:63). There is no doubt that the Spirit here refers to life. This Spirit is not a matter of person but of life. In other words, the Spirit here is not with respect to making decisions but with respect to supplying.

The Spirit is life to be our supply. Some passages, however, refer to the Spirit with the emphasis on the person and not on life. For example: "But he who is joined to the Lord is one spirit" (1 Cor. 6:17). The emphasis concerning the Spirit in this passage is not on life but on a person; the emphasis is not on life's supplying, but on a person's leading and making decisions.

We admit that this point is new to us. I fully believe that in the past we did not have this utterance, that the Spirit is, on the one hand, life to us and, on the other hand, a person to us. In the past we spoke something about life being in the Spirit, and we also spoke about the Spirit being the person of the Lord. Jesus is the name, and the Spirit is the person. When we call, "Lord Jesus," the Spirit comes; we immediately get the Spirit. At the same time, when this Spirit enters us, He becomes our life. Although we have spoken about these things, the light has never been as clear as it is today. Today we can clearly see that with respect to the Body, the Spirit is life, and with respect to the new man, this Spirit is a person. One Body, one new man, and one Spirit. This one Spirit is the life of the Body and the person of the new man.

First Corinthians 12:13 says that whether Jews or Greeks, whether slaves or free, we were all baptized into one Body. Where were we baptized? In one Spirit. In one Spirit we were all baptized into one Body. Furthermore, we were all given to drink one Spirit. This passage refers to the Spirit twice: once for baptism and once for drinking. Baptism is our being put into this Spirit, and drinking is our getting this Spirit into us. The emphasis here is not on the Spirit as a person but as life.

Another portion, Philippians 1:19, speaks of the bountiful supply of the Spirit of Jesus Christ. You must admit that this refers to the Spirit as a person. Since it is He who comes to supply us, it is not just a matter of life but of person.

We must be clear that for both the Body and the new man, what we need is this Spirit. Without the Spirit, the Body is short of life and the new man is short of a person.

THE PROBLEM WITH TODAY'S CHRISTIANITY

The problem with today's Christianity is that many do not

know the Spirit in a proper way. Christianity teaches that God is three persons—the Holy Father, the Holy Son, and the Holy Spirit—in one Body. I was clear about this doctrine from my childhood, but I had no experience of the Holy Spirit. *The Holy Spirit* was a term, *the Holy Son* was a term, and *the Holy Father* was also a term. These are the three terms for the Triune God. This is the teaching of the old, orthodox Christianity. Gradually, the Pentecostal movement came in with another way of teaching that confused people even more. According to the Pentecostal people, it does not matter whether you speak of the Holy Spirit or the Spirit of God. They say that if you speak in tongues, you have the Holy Spirit, and if you do not speak in tongues, you do not have the Holy Spirit. I also experienced the Pentecostal movement, and at that time I even led people, taught people, and encouraged people to speak in tongues. When I look back on those tongue-speakings, they were always, "Duh, duh, duh," or "Dee, dee, dah." What are these so-called tongues? Only the Lord knows.

In any case, we cannot approve of this kind of tongue-speaking. In addition, throughout history there have been millions of people who really had life and power yet never spoke in tongues. Many people were truly helped by Brother Watchman Nee, and I served the Lord beside him. He clearly told me that he had never spoken in tongues. Furthermore, in 1936 when he heard that I was in Tientsin speaking in tongues and leading others to speak in tongues, he immediately sent me a telegram from Shanghai. The telegram had neither a salutation nor a complimentary close; it contained only one sentence: "Not all speak in tongues." As soon as I read it, I understood. It is true that not all speak in tongues, and he himself never spoke in tongues. Can you say that one such as he did not have the Holy Spirit? You cannot say this.

We must leave the teachings of this group or that group in Christianity; there are too many teachings. Early on in the second and third centuries there were great battles over the ways to speak about the truths of the Trinity, and in the end there were the church councils and synods to discuss how to resolve these disagreements. In the past thirty to fifty

years this battle has been going on. Because the old tradi-
tional teaching concerning the Father, Son, and Holy Spirit
was too doctrinal, dead, and non-experiential, it brought in a
reaction called the Pentecostal movement. This reaction
began in the past century around the year 1850. At the beginning the reaction was wild with jumping, rolling, and many
other things. More recently this movement has become a
movement of spiritual gifts, and it is more cultured and
more moderate without the laughing, jumping, and rolling.
However, the focus is on this one thing: If you speak in
tongues, you have the Holy Spirit, and if you do not speak
in tongues, you do not have the Holy Spirit. You can see the
two extremes in Christianity: One is to teach empty doctrines, and the other is to promote speaking in tongues.

CHRISTIANITY'S LACK OF KNOWLEDGE
CONCERNING THE SPIRIT
AND THE THINGS THAT WE HAVE SEEN

Because of the dead doctrines on one side and the wild
Pentecostal things on the other, we were led to the Bible to
make a thorough study. I can tell you that over the past fifty
years there have been two topics which we studied the most.
The first is the church; in these fifty years we have been very
clear concerning the revelation of the church. The second is
the Holy Spirit. In these years I do not know how much time
we have spent studying the Spirit. We read and studied the
Bible again and again, and we have gotten clear about almost
every passage in the Bible that refers to the Spirit. Moreover,
we can say that we have consulted almost every great school
of teaching from the second century up through the present to
see their explanation and understanding of the Holy Spirit.
From this we have discovered that two things are lacking in
the discussions concerning the Spirit throughout the centuries.

First, there is the lack of the knowledge of how the Lord in
His death and resurrection became the life-giving Spirit. No
one taught clearly enough on this point. In the past it seems
that this was something seen uniquely among us and that we
may have been the only ones to tell people about it. Anyone

who has been with us for some time knows that we did not have the utterance for this in mainland China. When we were in mainland China, prior to 1949, the books we put out did not have this teaching, that the last Adam became a life-giving Spirit. Nor did we release any messages on this topic. It was only after coming to Taiwan that we began to emphasize that when our Lord Jesus Christ died and then entered into resurrection, He became a life-giving Spirit in resurrection. In these last three to five years, however, we discovered that in the past and even up to the present, there have been many great Bible expositors who have said the same thing. Some said that in resurrection Christ and the Holy Spirit are equal; some said that in resurrection Christ is the Spirit of power. These points have been seen, but throughout the centuries no one has sufficiently emphasized or developed them.

Second, prior to us there may never have been anyone who paid adequate attention to the seven Spirits in Revelation. Today we not only see that the Holy Spirit is part of the Triune God—the Holy Father, the Holy Son, and the Holy Spirit—nor do we only see the Spirit of Pentecost who enables people to have the manifestation of different gifts, including speaking in tongues—but we also see that the resurrected Christ is the life-giving Spirit and that in the darkest hour of the church age this Spirit has become the sevenfold intensified Spirit. God—the Father, the Son, and the Spirit—is triune. Doctrinally-speaking this is absolutely correct. Furthermore, on the day of Pentecost when the Holy Spirit was poured out, people did receive gifts and spoke in tongues. This, too, is correct. However, it is not sufficient to see only these two matters; we must go on to see that the resurrected Christ is the life-giving Spirit in resurrection. On the one hand, the Lord resurrected and ascended to the heavens, but on the other hand, He remained on the earth after His resurrection. From the aspect of ascension, He has already been made both Lord and Christ. From the aspect of remaining on the earth, He is the life-giving Spirit in resurrection. In the heavens He is the Lord, and on the earth He is the life-giving Spirit. This involves a great deal more than His simply being the Holy Spirit and the One giving gifts at

Pentecost. Furthermore, today in the church's darkest hour He is the sevenfold intensified Spirit, the seven Spirits before the throne of God. We must add up all four of these aspects: the Holy Spirit is the Spirit of Pentecost, the Spirit of Pentecost is the life-giving Spirit, and the life-giving Spirit is the seven Spirits.

What is our conclusion? Our conclusion is that today this Triune God is the very Spirit. In this Spirit there is the Holy Father; in this Spirit there is the Holy Son; in this Spirit there is the Holy Spirit; in this Spirit there is divinity; in this Spirit there is the uplifted, resurrected humanity; in this Spirit there is the Lord Jesus' all-inclusive death with its efficacy; and in this Spirit there is His resurrection with its power. In this Spirit there are all the glory of divinity and all the virtues of humanity.

This Spirit is what the New Testament calls "the Spirit." John 7:39 says, "But this He said concerning the Spirit, whom those who believed into Him were about to receive; for the Spirit was not yet, because Jesus had not yet been glorified." Ephesians 4:3 says, "Being diligent to keep the oneness of the Spirit." The Spirit spoken of in these passages is the Holy Spirit, the Spirit of Pentecost, the life-giving Spirit, and the sevenfold intensified Spirit. When we speak about one Body, one new man, and one Spirit, the one Spirit refers to *the Spirit*. The Spirit is life with respect to the Body of Christ, and the Spirit is the person with respect to the new man. The Spirit is the life of the Body and also the person of the new man.

THE SECRET TO ENJOYING THE SPIRIT

My burden at this time is on how to enjoy the Spirit. The secret to enjoying the Spirit is found in 1 Corinthians 12:13. We all must believe that we have experienced the first half of 1 Corinthians 12:13. In one Spirit, that is, in *the Spirit,* we were all baptized into one Body, whether Jews or Greeks. The Spirit and the Body are connected. We must believe that we believers of the Lord were in that one Spirit baptized into one Body. Do you believe that you are in the Body today? Since you believe that you are in the Body, then you must also

believe that you are in the Spirit. It does not matter whether
or not you speak in tongues. Do not be bothered by this point.
The fact is that all of us believers in the Lord have been baptized in one Spirit into one Body.

Today the problem is with the second part of 1 Corinthians
12:13: "And were all given to drink one Spirit." The Greek text
here is very difficult to translate. The meaning of the original
language is that you have been placed in a position to drink.
It is as if there is a drinking fountain outside, and you bring
me to it and set me in the right position. Then I am enabled to
drink from that drinking fountain. From the first day that
we were baptized into the Body, we were placed in a position
in which we were given to drink one Spirit. We all have the
position to drink the Spirit.

Anyone can tell from reading 1 Corinthians 12:13 that it is
not a small verse but a great verse in the Bible. We have all
been baptized into the Spirit, and now we need to drink this
Spirit. Drinking is the way we receive Him. We have already
been baptized into the Body and have been put in this position, so now we need to drink.

The problem in Christianity is that many people think too
much and do not drink enough. The theology and teaching in
Christianity are all on thinking, not on drinking. However, I
have found a secret: I do not need to think, study, discuss, or
quote the Bible; I simply drink. Consider a glass of water.
No matter how much you try to study, analyze, and describe
the water, not even the scientists among us who may have
written ten books on the subject can give a clear explanation
of what water is. Moreover, the scientists may eventually
divide into different groups and fight among themselves.
When I drink from a glass and take the water into my being,
my thirst is quenched and I am strengthened, but not even
someone with five Ph.Ds is able to research, discuss this
glass of water, and clearly explain it. If the tiny human brain
cannot explain a simple glass of water, how can it thoroughly
explain the Holy Spirit, the Spirit of Pentecost, and the sevenfold intensified Spirit? It is impossible.

I exhort you all not to think, discuss, or write about drinking; simply come to drink. Here is the easiest way: Come to

drink the glass of water. I am afraid that you may go out to speak about the water, but none of you will drink the water. You do not get a drink by talking about it, nor do you get a drink by understanding it or by speaking about it correctly. I could be a country person who cannot say anything correctly, but I can constantly drink this water. Let us all drink this water!

THE WAY TO DRINK THE SPIRIT

How do we drink? We simply need to call, "O Lord Jesus!" It is that simple. You may oppose and argue, but if you do not drink in this way, you will not get a drink. Just try it and see. Let us all leave our position as "scholars" and be "country folks," living the "country life" and drinking together. If your drinking is too refined, you will not enjoy the taste much. On the other hand, uneducated country people often enjoy their drinking. I would urge everyone not to care about being polite when eating the spiritual feast; simply care for the enjoyment by tasting its sweetness and eating to your heart's content.

From our experience, we have discovered that if you do not call on the Lord's name, you will probably not get a drink of the living water. We have all been given to drink the one Spirit. I would ask you, have you drunk yet? How much have you drunk? Do you drink daily? I can certainly testify that since the day I saw this, I have realized that I cannot get by without drinking.

Do not ever consider that calling on the Lord's name is a small matter. It is a great matter! In our physical body, breathing is a crucial matter. In the spiritual things, if you have the experience, you will understand that drinking is breathing, breathing is drinking, and drinking is eating. Have you heard this kind of speaking before? Breathing is drinking, and drinking is eating. What is breathing? It is calling on the name of the Lord, as in *Hymns,* #73, stanza two, which says, "Blessed Jesus! Mighty Savior! / In Thy Name is all I need; / Just to breathe the Name of Jesus, / Is to drink of Life indeed." For us to breathe is just to drink, and to drink is just to eat. A baby eats by drinking milk; his drinking is his eating. We all must understand that our calling on the Lord today is our breathing the Lord, our breathing the Lord is our drinking the Lord, and our drinking the Lord is our eating the Lord. When we breathe much, that is our drinking; and when we drink much, that is our eating. All we need to do is call on the Lord's name, and we simultaneously drink and eat. The result is that we receive air, water, and food. When a person receives air, water, and food, will he not be healthy?

I remember clearly that twenty years ago the Lord began to recover among us the matters of exercising our spirit, using our spirit, releasing our spirit, and eating, drinking, and enjoying the Lord. In the spring of 1958, in this very place, we had three conferences in a row for two weeks each in which we spoke about eating, drinking, and enjoying God. From that time until today, we have spoken more and more on this topic, and the more we speak, the more we have to speak. I believe that this teaching will increase more and more among us because this is our most critical personal need. If as co-workers and responsible brothers in the churches you do not know how to breathe, drink, eat, and enjoy the Lord, you will never be able to make the churches in your localities living.

THE PROPER CONDITION OF THE CHURCHES

Dear brothers and sisters, I do not approve of screaming, shouting, and making much noise. However, I also do not agree with the old Christianity way in which everyone comes at the scheduled time clutching a Bible to have a worship service, and while waiting for the pastor to come, each one greets this friend and that friend. If you want me to go back to support this, I cannot do it, even if you were to threaten me with beheading. This practice kills people, and I do not want to be an "executioner." Nor do I encourage you to scream, shout, leap, or jump. However, if we keep pace with the Lord's recovery by constantly calling on the Lord in spirit, breathing the Lord, drinking the Lord, and eating the Lord, then we will daily partake of Him and experience Him as our living water and our Companion. If all of us here at this time, more than ten thousand people, were the "living creatures" and if we were to live this way to such an extent that even the universe would be startled, then all the demons would flee from us. We may use this conference as an example. The way of Christianity is that each denomination first sends representatives to a joint planning session in which the leader of the conference is chosen and the methods are discussed. Then they put advertisements in all the newspapers. In the conference meetings everything is done according to rituals, and the atmosphere is dead. In the church, however, if everyone is burning inwardly by eating, drinking, and breathing the Lord, then we, like Benjamin, as ravenous wolves, will tear the devil to pieces. Whenever we are living, the demons immediately flee. When we sing hymns, there are not even any shadows, but all are in life, and the angels in the air shout for joy. I tell you that anyone who comes into such a situation will be saved. Everyone is enlivened because death will have already been swallowed up by the life of the church. I deeply feel that the church in each locality should have such a condition.

I would only ask that when you get into life and have this living, you would please avoid natural activities. We do not want to have any activities in the flesh. We want our spirits to be strong, living, and released. I definitely know that calling on the Lord will change us, but you should not shout early in the morning when the neighbors are still sleeping. This is neither ethical nor righteous. Our voices should not be thrust on others. We can call on the Lord Jesus softly, gently, and quietly. Also when we come together for morning watch, we should not disturb others with our loud pray-reading of the Word and our calling on the Lord's name. We should always exercise heavenly wisdom; the new man should have the wisdom of the new man.

THE SCRIPTURAL BASIS
FOR CALLING ON THE NAME OF THE LORD

My point is that you should not forget that we all must drink the Spirit. There is no other way to drink the Spirit except by calling on the name of the Lord. Calling on the Lord is absolutely scriptural; it has a basis in the Bible. First

Corinthians 12:3 says, "No one can say, Jesus is Lord! except in the Holy Spirit." Thus, even if you reverse the order of the name, when you say, "Jesus is Lord," you are in the Spirit. As soon as you open your mouth and breathe, the air gets into you. Today the Spirit is the living air, so all you need to do is call on the Lord's name: "O Lord Jesus!" Then you will immediately feel that within you there is some fresh air. This is not something psychological. If you call on Socrates, Washington, or Lincoln, nothing will happen. However, when you call on the Lord Jesus, something happens. Even if you call on Him in a joking way, six out of ten times you will be touched by the Lord. If you were to call on all the famous people from the past to the present, you could call for half a day, but the more you call, the more thirsty you will become, because those names do not give water or breath. However, when you call, "O Lord Jesus!" you will be completely changed. If you call a few more times, your tears will well up. "O Lord Jesus, You are so good and so sweet. I love You." We can all experience this.

If you go back and reread both the Old and New Testaments, you will discover that there are several hundred records of calling on the Lord. The verses on calling that I treasure the most are Lamentations 3:55-56: "I called upon Your name, O Jehovah, / From the lowest pit. / ...do not hide / Your ear at my breathing." This clearly tells us that calling on the Lord is our breathing. Both the Body and the new man depend on breathing the Lord's name. When we call on the Lord's name and drink the Spirit, the Spirit is life to the Body and the person to the new man. It is by enjoying the Lord in this way that all the saints on the entire earth can become one new man.

Chapter Ten

THE SPIRIT AND THE SEVEN SPIRITS

Scripture Reading: Rev. 1:4; 2:7, 11, 17, 26-29; 3:5-6, 12-13, 21-22; 14:13; 22:17

REVELATION BEING A BOOK ON THE SPIRIT AND THE CHURCHES

In this message we come to Revelation, which is the last book of the Bible. From the time I was saved, I loved to read the Bible, and I loved understanding the Bible even more. From my youth I began to pay attention to the book of Revelation. Later I heard many expositions on Revelation and read many books expounding this book. Some emphasized the numbers, while others emphasized the prophecies; some were historical, others were dispensational, and still others were doctrinal. However, after hearing and reading these things and after having quite a number of years of experience in the church, the Lord Himself eventually showed me that this book is not a book of prophecies, numbers, history, dispensations, or doctrines. Rather, this book is on the Spirit and the churches. In its very beginning, it says, "John to the seven churches which are in Asia:...from Him who is and who was and who is coming, and from the seven Spirits who are before His throne" (1:4). The seven epistles were written from the seven Spirits to the seven churches. Immediately in chapter one the seven Spirits and the seven churches are shown. Here we see that the seven churches need the seven Spirits: How they deal with things, how they have their living, how they bear the testimony, and how they go on, all depend on the seven Spirits. The seven churches need the seven Spirits, and the seven Spirits are for the seven churches.

However, if you have spent some years in Christianity, you can testify that Christianity does not touch the seven Spirits, nor does it touch the seven churches. Many there avoid speaking on the book of Revelation with the result that in Christianity today Revelation is not a revealed book but a veiled one. We thank the Lord, however, that in these years the Lord has certainly removed the veil from us. This book of the Bible has truly become a revelation; it is not covered but revealed. Over these past few years, the thing that has made me the happiest is the fact that the entire New Testament from the first page of Matthew to the last page of Revelation is as clear as crystal to us. Particularly in the last pages of Revelation is the light especially bright. The light is shining on these two points: the seven Spirits and the seven churches. Simply put, the shining brightness of this book lies with the Spirit and the churches. In chapters two and three, seven times in a row it says that he who has an ear should hear what the Spirit says to the churches. Then at the end of chapter twenty-two, it says that the Spirit and the bride say, "Come." In the beginning the Spirit is the Spirit and the seven churches are the seven churches. But at the end, the Spirit and the bride are one. The Spirit's saying, "Come!" is the bride's saying, "Come," and the bride's saying, "Come!" is the Spirit's saying, "Come."

THE SPIRIT IN REVELATION

There is yet another marvelous matter; that is, in Revelation we cannot find the title *Holy Spirit;* it is not mentioned even once. The book of Revelation speaks of either the seven Spirits or *the Spirit.* We cannot find the title *the Holy Spirit.* Due to their old concepts, the people who translated the Chinese version of the Bible did not include in their translation the word *the* in the term *the Spirit.* The Bible does not use words carelessly. In Genesis, the first book of the Bible, when it first mentions the Spirit of God, it does not say "the Holy Spirit" or "the Spirit"; it says that "the Spirit of God" was brooding upon the surface of the waters. Later there is the term *the Spirit of Jehovah,* but it still does not say "the Spirit" or "the Holy Spirit." In the Old Testament there are "the

Spirit of God" and "the Spirit of Jehovah," but there is not yet "the Holy Spirit." Some translations may use the term "Holy Spirit," but that is an inaccurate translation. There is not yet the term "Holy Spirit" in the Old Testament. The term "Holy Spirit" is not used until the incarnation of the Lord Jesus. The "Holy Spirit" is a New Testament term to describe the Spirit of God. But eventually in the New Testament, "the Spirit" appears. "But this He said concerning the Spirit, whom those who believed into Him were about to receive; for the Spirit was not yet" (John 7:39). By the time of Revelation, the Spirit had been there for a long time, and furthermore, the Spirit became the sevenfold intensified Spirit. This sevenfold intensified Spirit cannot be found in Genesis, Matthew, Acts, or even the Epistles. It is in Revelation that the Spirit becomes the sevenfold intensified Spirit. Today we are neither in Genesis nor in Matthew; we are even beyond the Epistles. Today we are in Revelation in the sevenfold intensified Spirit. The Spirit of God, the Holy Spirit, and the life-giving Spirit are the Spirit in us.

We all know that the Spirit is especially rich and all-inclusive, with an abundantly rich supply. Ephesians 4 speaks of one Body and one Spirit, and this one Spirit is *the Spirit*. Impoverished Christianity has not seen that the Spirit of God is the Spirit, who is the all-inclusive Spirit. As the Spirit, He is both in us and outside of us. This Spirit is not only the Holy Spirit; He is also the Son and the Father. He is the Triune God. In this Spirit there is not only divinity but also humanity. This Spirit passed through incarnation, put on humanity, and lived on earth for thirty-three and a half years. He entered into death, and in death He solved all the negative problems and met all God's demands. He passed through death and has with Him the effectiveness of death; He resurrected and has with Him the power and the freshness of resurrection. He is Lord, He is God, and He possesses the resurrected and uplifted humanity. He has the glory of God and the virtues of man. This One is referred to in the Bible as *the Spirit*. In the New Testament there are many symbols of the Spirit. For example, the Spirit is like air for us to breathe, like water for us to drink, like wind that is full of power, and like a mantle for us to put on.

We have said that this Spirit is our life with respect to the Body of Christ and our person with respect to the new man that God wants. Our regenerated spirit and the Spirit can be mingled into one spirit. This is a marvelous thing. I would like to tell you that for the Lord to obtain His Body and gain the one new man on earth today, we need to realize that this is altogether a matter in the Spirit, not in doctrines, regulations, or practices. Moreover, this Spirit today is not high above us so that He is unreachable; rather, He is in our spirit. The Spirit is in our spirit today.

THE BOOK OF REVELATION
BEING CLOSED TO CHRISTIANITY
BUT OPENED TO THE CHURCHES

Poor Christianity has degraded into a religion that pays attention only to outward actions and outward corrections. I can truthfully say that through our Chinese heritage we all understand ethics and morality, and we all know how to improve ourselves. Concerning self-improvement and ethics or morality, the books written by Confucius and Mencius are already sufficient. In my youth I was born into Christianity, and at first I loved and defended Christianity until one day I heard a Western pastor say that Christianity teaches us to honor our parents, to respect our elder brothers, to be upright, and to be honest, just as what Confucius taught. This caused me to question Christianity, and my heart became cold. The Western missionaries did not know enough about God's economy and about the Spirit in God's economy. They saw only the things in the Bible which matched their concepts. When they read Ephesians, they never found the truth of the spirit of wisdom and revelation, nor did they discover that the church is the fullness of the One who fills all in all. They could see that chapter five tells wives to submit to their husbands and husbands to love their wives, and they could also see that you must be humble and that you must honor your parents. But concerning the verses on the one Body, being members one of another, and putting off the old man and putting on the new man, of which we have been speaking, they could not understand, and they would not touch them. Some of them even said that the Bible is not for man to thoroughly understand, so one should read only whatever he can understand, and whatever he cannot understand, he should just let it go. This has been the pitiful condition of Christianity in the past.

We praise and thank the Lord that today the Bible before us is not like this. Today the depths of the Bible are shining before our eyes. We know the church is His Body, the fullness of the One who fills all in all. We know what the church is, what the Body is, what the fullness is, what being filled is, and what is meant by the word *all*. We also know the one new man and the one Spirit. We know the all-inclusive Spirit, the Spirit, the seven Spirits, and the life-giving Spirit. Today the Bible is so clear, and the book of Revelation is truly revealed and not concealed anymore. I know this is the Lord's marvelous work in His sovereignty.

I would like to say again that I am so happy that I can see the second generation, numbering even thousands, in the churches. There are young people rising up everywhere. Moreover, the light of the truth at this time is clear and bright. When we began the work here twenty-nine years ago, we did not have such clear light. We did not understand the life-giving Spirit, the sevenfold intensified Spirit, or the matter of eating the Lord to live by Him, but now the younger generation understands all these things. Therefore, I have the confidence that all these precious truths will be released quickly to the entire earth. Let the denominations oppose us today, but in ten years many may speak our language. This is because what is good is good, and what is superior is superior. Today we are here speaking about one Body, one Spirit, and one new man. In five years, those outside the Lord's recovery will also speak about one Body, one Spirit, and one new man. The Lord will prevail.

THOSE WITH EARS TO HEAR
WHAT THE SPIRIT SPEAKS TO THE CHURCHES
BECOMING OVERCOMERS

Now I would like to show you that Revelation 2 and 3 speak

again and again about what the overcomers must do and how those with an ear must hear what the Spirit is speaking to the churches. This word includes four things: first, the Spirit; second, the churches; third, those with ears (those who can hear); and fourth, the overcomers. One day a young brother asked me, "We in the local churches realize that we must be the new man. Then what about those who are in the denominations? What should our attitude be about them?" I would like to answer this question here. We must know this one principle in the Bible: When the majority of God's people have failed God and cannot meet His need, God calls a small number of overcomers. You must see that even though the Spirit is speaking to the churches, not everyone in the churches will follow closely; therefore, there is the call for the overcomers. Although the word spoken by the Spirit is to all the churches, the Bible also says that whoever has an ear let him hear. If you hear it, you will be an overcomer. I am not saying that everyone in the local churches in the Lord's recovery is an overcomer. I dare not say this. However, everyone in the churches today can easily have an ear to hear. Today many in the denominations oppose the Spirit's speaking. Those in the local churches, however, listen respectfully instead of opposing. "O Lord, speak, and we will hear." We are here in a position to hear the Spirit's speaking, and we can easily have ears. Now I am happy because I know that almost everyone here has an ear to hear. We all have ears that can hear. We have the Spirit and the churches, and we also have ears to hear. As a result, the overcomers will be produced.

Today our attitude toward Christians is that we are broad and loving. We are blunt in speaking of Christianity because the "anity" is a bad thing, but despite this fact we love the Christians. We must distinguish Christianity from Christians. Regardless of what denomination Christians are in, even if they are in Catholicism, they are still the believers and our brothers. But the religion, the organization, is not of God. What we criticize, condemn, and oppose is the "anity" or religion. We do not oppose Christ; we oppose the "anity." Neither do we oppose the Christians; we love our brothers and sisters. It does not matter what denomination they are in, we love them. It does not matter how much they oppose us; we still love them because they are children of God. However, you must remember that it is one thing to sympathize with them, and it is another thing to be faithful. Today many do not have an ear to hear, but you have an ear, so you cannot listen in the same way they listen; you need to overcome. Whoever has an ear to hear what the Spirit speaks to the churches should hear and then be an overcomer.

At this time I cannot tell you in detail what the overcomers are, but if you read through Revelation 2 and 3, the condition of the overcomers and the requirements for overcoming will be shown to you. When you overcome, you can enjoy Christ as the tree of life and as the manna, and you can become a white stone as the material for God's building. When you overcome, you can be a pillar in the temple of God. When you overcome, you can wear white garments and walk with the Lord. When you overcome, one day you will have authority to reign with the Lord and rule over the nations. By what way do the overcomers come? They come by having ears to hear. The ear to hear is produced through the Spirit's speaking to the churches. All those with an ear should hear what the Spirit speaks to the churches, and those who hear will be overcomers.

THE PROPER CONDITION OF THE OVERCOMERS

Brothers and sisters, in conclusion I would like to say that if you would like to be a top Christian, you must be a Christian in the churches of the Lord's recovery. You must also learn to live in the Body and not ever be individualistic. Furthermore, you must also understand that the churches in the Lord's recovery on the entire earth are just one new man. Never be individualistic, and never be divisive; instead, be in the one Body and in the one new man. Moreover, in everything and in every matter in your living you must also continuously follow what the Spirit within you is speaking to the churches. Simply put, you must follow the Spirit, live in the Body, and live in the new man. This is our way today. Whatever would cause you to be separated from the Body is heretical. Whatever would cause you not to live in the new man is also an error. Whatever is not spoken by the Spirit within you is conceived only in your own mind. We must see the one Body, the one Spirit, and the one new man. We all need to hear what the Spirit within us is speaking to the churches today.

Moreover, we should always live in the Body, never being individualistic. We should never separate from the Body or divide the Body. Instead, we should continuously live in the new man. By this way I believe there will be a ninety percent possibility that we can be overcomers. One Body and one new man and one Spirit. We should always listen to and follow the Spirit.

From now on there should not be doctrinal disputes among us, nor should there be arguments about insignificant matters or anything outward. We should all simply seek to arrive at the oneness of the faith, endeavoring to keep the oneness of the Spirit. We should listen to and follow the Spirit. We do not listen to mere objective doctrines; instead, we listen to what the subjective Spirit speaks within us. We should absolutely not be individualistic, divisive, or separated from that one new man. This is our way, and this is the Lord's testimony. I believe that after this training, the Lord's word will begin to operate in all the localities, and His light will shine brightly in every place. Our younger generation will aggressively develop these truths and bring all the children of God into the voice of the Spirit that they may live in the Body and have the living of the one new man together. In this way the Lord's purpose will be accomplished and His heart's desire will be satisfied. I believe that this will bring the Lord back.

ABOUT THE AUTHOR

Witness Lee was born in 1905 in northern China and raised in a Christian family. At age 19 he was fully captured for Christ and immediately consecrated himself to preach the gospel for the rest of his life. Early in his service, he met Watchman Nee, a renowned preacher, teacher, and writer. Witness Lee labored together with Watchman Nee under his direction. In 1934 Watchman Nee entrusted Witness Lee with the responsibility for his publication operation, called the Shanghai Gospel Bookroom.

Prior to the Communist takeover in 1949, Witness Lee was sent by Watchman Nee and his other co-workers to Taiwan to insure that the things delivered to them by the Lord would not be lost. Watchman Nee instructed Witness Lee to continue the former's publishing operation abroad as the Taiwan Gospel Bookroom, which has been publicly recognized as the publisher of Watchman Nee's works outside China. Witness Lee's work in Taiwan manifested the Lord's abundant blessing. From a mere 350 believers, newly fled from the mainland, the churches in Taiwan grew to 20,000 in five years.

In 1962 Witness Lee felt led of the Lord to come to the United States, settling in California. During his 35 years of service in the U.S., he ministered in weekly meetings and weekend conferences, delivering several thousand spoken messages. Much of his speaking has since been published as over 400 titles. Many of these have been translated into over fourteen languages. He gave his last public conference in February 1997 at the age of 91.

He leaves behind a prolific presentation of the truth in the Bible. His major work, *Life-study of the Bible,* comprises over 25,000 pages of commentary on every book of the Bible from the perspective of the believers' enjoyment and experience of God's divine life in Christ through the Holy Spirit. Witness Lee was the chief editor of a new translation of the New Testament into Chinese called the Recovery Version and directed the translation of the same into English. The Recovery Version also appears in a number of other languages. He provided an extensive body of footnotes, outlines, and spiritual cross references. A radio broadcast of his messages can be heard on Christian radio stations in the United States. In 1965 Witness Lee founded Living Stream Ministry, a non-profit corporation, located in Anaheim, California, which officially presents his and Watchman Nee's ministry.

Witness Lee's ministry emphasizes the experience of Christ as life and the practical oneness of the believers as the Body of Christ. Stressing the importance of attending to both these matters, he led the churches under his care to grow in Christian life and function. He was unbending in his conviction that God's goal is not narrow sectarianism but the Body of Christ. In time, believers began to meet simply as the church in their localities in response to this conviction. In recent years a number of new churches have been raised up in Russia and in many eastern European countries.

OTHER BOOKS PUBLISHED BY
Living Stream Ministry

Titles by Witness Lee:

Abraham—Called by God	0-7363-0359-6
The Experience of Life	0-87083-417-7
The Knowledge of Life	0-87083-419-3
The Tree of Life	0-87083-300-6
The Economy of God	0-87083-415-0
The Divine Economy	0-87083-268-9
God's New Testament Economy	0-87083-199-2
The World Situation and God's Move	0-87083-092-9
Christ vs. Religion	0-87083-010-4
The All-inclusive Christ	0-87083-020-1
Gospel Outlines	0-87083-039-2
Character	0-87083-322-7
The Secret of Experiencing Christ	0-87083-227-1
The Life and Way for the Practice of the Church Life	0-87083-785-0
The Basic Revelation in the Holy Scriptures	0-87083-105-4
The Crucial Revelation of Life in the Scriptures	0-87083-372-3
The Spirit with Our Spirit	0-87083-798-2
Christ as the Reality	0-87083-047-3
The Central Line of the Divine Revelation	0-87083-960-8
The Full Knowledge of the Word of God	0-87083-289-1
Watchman Nee—A Seer of the Divine Revelation ...	0-87083-625-0

Titles by Watchman Nee:

How to Study the Bible	0-7363-0407-X
God's Overcomers	0-7363-0433-9
The New Covenant	0-7363-0088-0
The Spiritual Man 3 volumes	0-7363-0269-7
Authority and Submission	0-7363-0185-2
The Overcoming Life	1-57593-817-0
The Glorious Church	0-87083-745-1
The Prayer Ministry of the Church	0-87083-860-1
The Breaking of the Outer Man and the Release ...	1-57593-955-X
The Mystery of Christ	1-57593-954-1
The God of Abraham, Isaac, and Jacob	0-87083-932-2
The Song of Songs	0-87083-872-5
The Gospel of God 2 volumes	1-57593-953-3
The Normal Christian Church Life	0-87083-027-9
The Character of the Lord's Worker	1-57593-322-5
The Normal Christian Faith	0-87083-748-6
Watchman Nee's Testimony	0-87083-051-1

Available at
Christian bookstores, or contact Living Stream Ministry
2431 W. La Palma Ave. • Anaheim, CA 92801
1-800-549-5164 • www.livingstream.com